Central Books – a brief history
1939 – 1999

CENTRAL BOOKS

a brief history

1939 to 1999

Dave Cope

Central Books Ltd

First published 1999 by Central Books Ltd
99 Wallis Road
London E9 5LN
tel 020 8986 4854

ISBN 0714732907

Cover illustration ALF Hoad
Cover and design by Suzanne Perkins/Grafica
Back cover photo of staff September 1999 by Leah Gordon
Printed by Redwood Books, Trowbridge, England

a brief introduction

Not many book distributors have survived for sixty years: books yes, authors yes, publishers yes, but distributors, no. Distributing is the most unglamorous part of the book trade – yes it might be necessary, but who's really interested? Storage, invoicing (and a bit of crediting), packing; collecting the money, keeping a little bit and passing the rest on to the publishers (even the books aren't ours) – it's no big deal. Perhaps not, but Central Books is no ordinary distributor. Central Books was set up by the Communist Party as its retail and wholesale outlet. The aim was to persuade the people of Britain, by the power of the written word, to join the cause of world revolution. Of course, this project was totally unsuccessful, but in its 70 years existence the Communist Party was active in many areas, making significant contributions to the trade union movement, anti-fascism, anti-colonialism, and to the world of the arts, among others. It attached great importance to its printing, publishing and distribution networks, producing books, pamphlets and leaflets on every conceivable topic. This belief in the power of the written word was unmatched by any other political organisation. In the course of serving this ideal, Central Books, surviving many crises of a financial, personnel and political nature, developed into a rather successful business and this trajectory is a story worth relating. And in the course of serving this same ideal (and later a few other ideals), many interesting and talented people (plus a few rogues) spent a good part of their working lives in Clerkenwell, Southwark and now Hackney picking and packing, invoicing and crediting, chasing debts and accounting, negotiating and marketing. This is the story of their sixty years and is dedicated to them. We hope it will be of some interest and entertainment to others in the booktrade, as well as those with an interest in left-wing politics.

This brief history started out as an oral history project and will link in with a more widespread one which is just starting up for the whole book trade. We were aware that people's memories were fading and that there were not many who would recall the earlier days of the company, so three of us – Dave Cope, Bill Norris and Gail Chester - selected a range of people of different ages and experiences and recorded their memories. We are grateful to those who agreed to be interviewed and hope this lives up to their expectations. We have tapes of interviews with the following: Reuben Falber, Charlie Hall, Pat Leppard, Arthur Mendelsohn, Bill Norris, Betty Reid, Dave Rosenberg, Mike Squires, and Iris Walker. Other people also responded with information. Apart from the interviews, the primary source used for this history was the minutes of the Board of Directors, which are almost all extant (all quotes are from these unless specified). I also referred to the many financial documents, reports for Board meetings, and 112 personnel records which were discovered by chance just in time to be used. All are kept at Central Books.

A brief note on the three interviewers: the two first named have spent practically all their working lives in the world of left-wing bookselling; Gail has many years experience in various aspects of the radical book trade and has made academic studies of this obscure chapter of the book world, together with more mainstream areas.

Thanks are due to Mike Squires for support and technical advice with the interviews, and to Sally Davison and Gail for comments on the text.

Of course, the author is solely responsible for all errors of fact, dodgy judgments and bad punctuation.

THE
COMMUNIST
BOOKSHOP
CATALOGUE

16, KING STREET, COVENT GARDEN,
LONDON, W. C. 2.
[TELEPHONE : GERRARD 877]

**Catalogues from
the early 1920s**

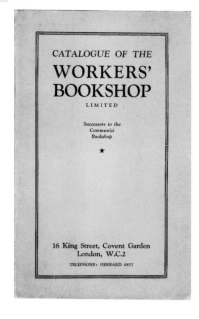

CATALOGUE OF THE
WORKERS'
BOOKSHOP
LIMITED

*Successors to the
Communist
Bookshop*

★

16 King Street, Covent Garden
London, W.C.2
TELEPHONE: GERRARD 0877

beginnings

The Communist Party of Great Britain was founded in 1920, and the following year the Communist Bookshop was opened in its headquarters at 16 King Street in Covent Garden, London. In 1927 there was a name change to Workers' Bookshop Ltd, and it was placed under the responsibility of Emile Burns, the CP's Press and Publicity supremo. The Workers' Bookshop acted as the CP's retail outlet, but it also distributed, from its inception, books and magazines - CP publications and Soviet journals, notably the Communist International's weekly *International Press Correspondence*, or *Inprecorr* as it was usually known. By 1930/1, Hymie Fagan was the manager, Florrie Bedford the bookkeeper (later replaced by Harry Bourne), and Charlie Hall the assistant who was also responsible for the Despatch Department; the shop was open daily from about 10.00 am – 6.00 pm and to 1.00 pm on Saturdays. It was probably late in 1933 that the Wholesale Department moved to Marx House in Clerkenwell Green – Charlie was in charge with one assistant.

Charlie Hall, born 1914, came from a political family (his father being a foundation member of the CP); he joined the YCL in 1930, having been a childhood member of the Young Comrades' League. Charlie worked for the *Workers' Illustrated News*, the *Sunday Worker*, and Martin Lawrence Ltd, the Party's publishing house, for a year before Harry Pollitt persuaded him to go to the Workers' Bookshop (late 1930/early 1931). Charlie was one of those Pollitt installed in the CP businesses after replacing Albert Inkpin at the head of the CP in 1929. Charlie participated in the 'Literature Commission' with Pollitt, and comrades from Martin Lawrence Ltd, the journals *Labour Research* and *Labour Monthly*, plus representatives from the Districts. This body made recommendations on what the Party should publish and how it should be distributed; it also published an interesting pamphlet, in 1938, entitled *Books and Pamphlets – How to Sell Them*, which describes in detail the whole process from writing to selling, almost as if it was a military campaign; surprisingly, it advises against setting up new bookshops, unless a huge amount of preparatory work had been completed. Charlie also recalls attending briefings after each Central Committee meeting with representatives from the other businesses. He served on the National Council of the Young Communist League. Charlie was refused permission to join the International Brigade when he applied, but Harry Bourne did leave the shop to go and fight in Spain, where he was injured.

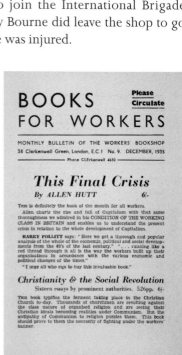

A monthly bulletin from The Workers' Bookshop

BOOKS FOR WORKERS

Please Circulate

MONTHLY BULLETIN OF THE WORKERS' BOOKSHOP
38 Clerkenwell Green, London, E.C.1   No. 9.   DECEMBER, 1935
Phone CLErkenwell 4610

This Final Crisis
By ALLEN HUTT   6/-

This is definitely the book of the month for all workers.

Allen charts the rise and fall of Capitalism with that same thoroughness we admired in his CONDITION OF THE WORKING CLASS IN BRITAIN and enables us to understand the present crisis in relation to the whole development of Capitalism.

HARRY POLLITT says: "Here we get a thorough and popular analysis of the whole of the economic, political and social developments from the 40's of the last century." ". . . running like a red thread through it all is the way the workers built up their organisations in accordance with the various economic and political changes of the times."

"I urge all who can to buy this invaluable book."

Christianity & the Social Revolution
Sixteen essays by prominent authorities. 526pp. 6/-

This book typifies the ferment taking place in the Christian Church to-day. Thousands of churchmen are revolting against the class nature of organised religion and are seeing their Christian ideals becoming realities under Communism. But the antipathy of Communism to religion puzzles them. This book should prove to them the necessity of fighting under the workers' banner.

While at the Workers' Bookshop, Charlie had the idea of setting up a left-wing book club based on the model of the American magazine *New Masses*, which distributed certain political books at a 'club' price. This was taken up and in 1935 the Workers' Bookshop asked John Strachey, a leading socialist academic, to be part of a selection committee; this went ahead and letters were sent to all publishers who had any left wing titles (Lawrence & Wishart – the successors to Martin Lawrence Ltd – was asked, but did not have the capital to finance a club on their own). Only Gollancz responded, and as nothing else happened Victor Gollancz went ahead on his own to launch the Left Book Club in 1936 [see Sheila Hodges *Gollancz – the Story of a Publishing House*, Gollancz 1978]. Workers' Bookshop acted as distributor for the Left Book Club, sending the distinctive, orange-covered monthly choices to members (this contract was later transferred to Collets). At this time Workers' Bookshop actually published a few pamphlets. On one occasion, Werner Laurie approached Charlie Hall with the manuscript of Upton Sinclair's novel *No Pasaran* asking for comments; as a result Workers' Bookshop published its own edition. Letterheads describe the company as: 'Wholesale and Export Booksellers; Publisher'. Central Books also, later on, acted as an occasional publisher, usually just as an English name for titles from the Soviet Union.

Charlie's other contribution to the radical booktrade at the time was when he was approached by the two old-timers of the Independent Labour Party, who ran Hendersons' 'Bomb Shop', the famous revolutionary bookshop in Charing Cross Road; they asked him if 'your lot' (i.e. the CP) wanted to take it over as they were retiring. Charlie reported back to Emile Burns; Eva Collet Reckitt, a wealthy Communist, stumped up the money, and Collets was founded. It was never an official CP bookshop, but the managers (Olive Parsons, Tom Russell, Joan Birch, Eva Skelley) were always in the CP and so were many of the staff. The shop continued its non-sectarian tradition of carrying a wide range of stock –

Anarchist, Communist, Trotskyist, Maoist etc. – and it became a unique feature not only of the Left, but also of the London booktrade, till it closed in the early 1990s.

Charlie Hall was the founder and chairman of the Central London Booksellers' branch of the Shop Assistants' Union, whose core membership came from Collets and Workers' Bookshop. (At the time of writing, in 1999, the current secretary of this branch of what is now USDAW, also works at Central Books). Charlie maintained his commitment to selling political books all his life: after he retired from teaching (his post-war career), among other activities he worked at the Marx Memorial Library between 1979 and 1982, and has long been involved in getting books donated to South African libraries, especially for the Communist Party and ANC; he is still doing this in 1999.

In January 1937, the Workers' Bookshop moved from Clerkenwell Green to 49 Farringdon Road. The Manager was Vernon (?) Littlewood; while Charlie was the buyer, and was also responsible for sales promotions (producing an irregular Bulletin), Charlie claims that he, not Littlewood, did most of the work. The staff expanded considerably at this time, mainly as a result of the contract to distribute the Left Book Club. Charlie remembers the daughters of George Lansbury, the Labour Party leader, and Arthur Horner, the leader of the South Wales' miners, working there, plus Ivy Macmillan and Anne Kelly. In July 1939, Workers' Bookshop was wound up – the Left Book Club was declining, political differences were emerging and there were cash flow problems. Reuben Falber recollects that 'they were unable to collect debts'. After Workers' Bookshop closed, the shop in King Street provided the sole retail outlet for the Party. Among those who worked in the shop in King Street were Jack Cohen, Pat Dooley, Glyn Evans, Harry Bourne (when he had sufficiently recovered from his injuries) and George Leeson, who had also been in the International Brigades and who was active in Unity Theatre.

In the same month, 'Central Publications' of 16 King Street was registered as a company by Charlie Hall. One of the reasons for the collapse of the Workers' Bookshop had been the large number of CP branches who had been supplied direct and who had not paid their bills; it was decided to re-organise the distribution apparatus, and send books and magazines to each Party District, who in turn would supply the branches – and the Districts had to pay in advance for part of their supplies. The name 'Central' was intended to reflect this re-structuring. The emphasis at this early stage was thus on distribution.

An advert in *The Daily Worker* on 31 December 1939 announced that from January 1st 1940 'the wholesale and retail business of Central Publications, 16 King Street, would be incorporated in Central Books Ltd'.

Central Books Ltd was officially registered in December 1939 – the original fading certificate is on the wall in our current premises in Hackney. The first directors were Robin Page Arnot, Clemens Palme Dutt, C Hall. The first allotment of shares was to: R P Arnot, William Clark (who edited the English version of *Inprecorr* with his wife, Bertha), C P Dutt, C Hall, and the Russia Today Society. Other early shareholders included: H Bourne, R Goodman, B Harvey, David Smith, L Milner ('Lieut. Commander R.N. Retired'), Joseph & Gertrude Armfield (described in the records as 'engineer' and 'married woman' respectively; their shares were held till transferred in 1985). Rodell Properties, the CP's business holding company, became a shareholder in August 1945. In 1940 a letter from the accountant to shareholders advised: 'It sometimes happens that in companies of a propaganda nature that share certificates get lost, especially where no value is attached to the shares, and it is suggested that if the shareholders do not particularly wish to hold the certificates, they should be left attached in the book.'

The advertisement in the *Daily Worker* announcing the new company

Wartime catalogue

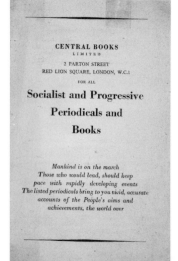

CENTRAL BOOKS
LIMITED

2 PARTON STREET
RED LION SQUARE, LONDON, W.C.1

FOR ALL

Socialist and Progressive Periodicals and Books

Mankind is on the march
Those who would lead, should keep
pace with rapidly developing events
The listed periodicals bring to you vivid, accurate
accounts of the People's aims and
achievements, the world over

the 1940s

In June 1940 Charlie Hall left Central Books – he was called up for military service - and Harry Bourne became manager (he was later a full-time CP worker). June also saw the first Directors' meeting, but there were only a handful of meetings till 1945, then they were monthly from March of that year.

Late in 1941, a very small shop had been opened on the ground floor of 2 Parton Street, on the corner of Red Lion Square: this was Central Books' first shop. It was in a building that housed the offices of Lawrence and Wishart, formed in 1936 from a merger of Martin Lawrence Ltd and Wishart Books. While there was certainly a Mr Wishart (who was sympathetic to the Communist Party, though his brother-in-law, Douglas Garman, was a noted literary figure who worked for the Party), it is thought that Martin Lawrence was a fictitious name. There was a Martin Lawrence, an opera singer and music critic, who was in the CP, but the company was not named after him; legend has it that the name was chosen for its initials, which referred to Marx and Lenin. The two companies shared these premises for a couple of years, before Lawrence and Wishart – often abbreviated to L&W for the sake of convenience – moved to Chancery Lane; surprisingly, it is not known whether L&W owned or rented Parton Street. Five decades later, in 1995, L&W were to move into Central's current premises. Central had been set up to distribute L&W's books, together with the CP's own pamphlets and journals, and the history of two companies is entwined, as we shall see.

In 1942, the Board of Directors' Minutes Book shows that Central raised money through personal loans to help expand; there is correspondence in the 1940s and 1950s about loans being repaid or being turned into gifts. Interest of 4% was paid on these loans, though this was sometimes waived by the lenders. Individuals and organisations who lent money included: the Association of Scientific Workers, Alan Bush the composer (in 1957 he wrote and 'expressed his desire to forgo repayment of his loan of £200'), William Hill the bookmaker (his brother-in-law was a trade union official and CP member) plus another bookmaker – Jimmy Shand from Liverpool. In October 1944, some lenders were sent a letter asking them to consider extending their loan by a year, to help pay for costs incurred in distributing The History of the CPSU as 10,000 copies had just arrived. This very official, Stalinist history, largely forgotten today, was the Soviet Communist Party's major text, and was faithfully sold in hundreds of thousands of copies by Communist Parties throughout the world. Analysts of Soviet politics would carefully check each new edition of this book for signs of policy and personnel changes.

Bagenal Harvey, the next manager of Central, on wages of £8 per week, offered to put an additional £5,000 into the company in April 1945; in June, David Smith and Joseph Moore put £2,500 into the company on becoming shareholders. It does seem that some of the earliest directors were chosen because they could put up some of their own money - they may have been less political appointments than those who followed. Smith was also a director of Hollywood Publications, Junior Press Ltd, Progress Publishing and D S Smith Ltd: he was a printer and box manufacturer based in Hatton Garden who moved to 37 Grays Inn Road in 1946 (and presumably at a later date he was linked to Central's move to this address). Moore was a director of A Warne Ltd, Junior Press Ltd, and Progress Publishing. Harvey was also a director of Junior Press and Progress Publishing (he also declared an interest in the *Irish Democrat* magazine). Central probably distributed Junior Press, Senior Press and Progress Publishing (which were, at least partially, political publishers); the company certainly distributed Hollywood Press titles. These other directorships may have led to a conflict of interest, as there are references in the minutes to stock and contract problems over some Hollywood Press titles. It is noteworthy that there was a director with experience of the outside publishing world – A Warne Ltd was a mainstream publisher.

Both Smith and Moore resigned as directors in March 1946 after only six months. Bagenal Harvey had resigned in February, officially due to ill-health ('on the verge of a nervous breakdown' according to the minutes); Charlie and others recall him leaving after a disagreement, probably to do with his policy of selling unusual books, i.e. non-political ones, and changing the image of the company without discussion. Reuben recalls a meeting of the CP's Central Organisation Committee at which Harry Pollitt was furious with Emile Burns for allowing this situation to develop. The whole episode is unclear from the minutes. David Smith did remain a member of the CP for years, often helping in fundraising. His shares in the company were only transferred in 1977 to the new manager. Occasionally shareholders would write in asking if their shares could be sold, but shares in Central were only ever nominal and of no value: new directors were usually given the shareholding of the retiring director they replaced, and to ensure that the Communist Party retained control of the company, any new director would sign, in advance, a resignation notice which was kept in the safe! This was probably the only way for the CP to ensure that any individual director, or even group of directors, could not remove the links with the Party, for instance after a political split. This procedure was never used – people resigned voluntarily. This marrying of business and politics will prove to be a recurring theme in this story. Incidentally, such problems over ownership of premises did arise from the 1970s, with the splits in the CP, but, up to then, the British CP was remarkable for the lack of organised factions and breakaways that characterised the world Communist movement.

Harvey appears to have been an unusual character and his future certainly took an unusual turn – he became an agent for various sportsmen, possibly acting for Dennis Compton and certainly acting for Johnny Haynes, who became the first footballer to earn £100 per week! Yet it does seem likely that he played an important role in establishing Central on a firm financial footing.

During 1944 and 1945, coinciding with the peak of Communist Party membership, Central Books expanded considerably; extra space for storage was rented in Charlotte Street, Southampton Place, and Gt. James Street, while the warehouse moved to 1 Doughty Street in November 1945. There was bomb damage to Parton Street at some stage during the war, but it is unclear how extensive this was (could it have been responsible for the move of Lawrence and Wishart?). One of the managers of the warehouse was George Cross, till he left to become secretary of the Ex-Service Movement for Peace; he also worked for the Party's travel agents, Progressive Tours. For this warehouse 'a number of table shelters and shelter bunks (i.e. from the war) had been purchased for adaptation as packing benches & storage bins. The cost was £52.10.0'. It is possible that one of these benches is still used today. Unfortunately, early in 1946 'The Secretary reported that since the transfer to Doughty St, a considerable number of complaints had been received from customers regarding the service rendered by the Company and that he was glad to report that the staff had set up a Committee which had been meeting regularly to work out internal organisational questions'.

At some stage during the war, the premises next door at

CENTRAL BOOKS

2-4 PARTON STREET, LONDON, W.C.1.

1944 SPRING LIST

4 Parton Street were also rented. This building deserves a brief history of its own. David Archer had a famous second-hand bookshop there, specialising in poetry and socialism, and was an early publisher of Dylan Thomas (who used to sleep in the attic); in the basement was Sidney Stanley, who published radical material including Esmond Romilly's revolutionary paper for public schools, *Out of Bounds*. In fact, the area was known for housing a plethora of left-leaning and bohemian businesses: Meg's Café, over the road, was a famous meeting place, and Freedom Books, the anarchist bookshop, was in Red Lion Passage at the opposite corner of Red Lion Square. This tradition went back some years, as in 1919 there had been H W Edwards' 'Progressive Bookshop' at 68 Red Lion Street (an early use of the word 'progressive' in the vocabulary of revolutionary enterprises – it was to be much more common after the Second World War).

The bookshop manager who is most remembered in this post war period is Henry Shelley; he worked there for many years till 1956; he ended up a successful businessman in the United States, still in publishing, and introduced himself to Central Books staff at their stall at the Frankfurt Bookfair in 1996.

Central also took over the CP's shop in Liverpool from the Lancashire District, accepting no liability for commitments, apart from trade debts of c£365; £50 was paid to the District, with stock estimated at £250; this was one of a number of attempts to help bookshops in the provinces though it was exceptional to run any from London. Dan Huxstep was appointed manager in Liverpool on a wage of £7 per week, plus 20% of net profits – though the wages were for both him and his wife, who also worked there.

In March 1946 Peter Wheeler was appointed MD on £8 wages plus £2 expenses. He was an accountant, married to Sheila Lynd (who had been a reader at Gollancz in the early days); during the war he had been a fighter pilot. He was perceived as upper middle class by Iris Walker, a future manager; 'he was a principled and competent organiser... not very political' according to Betty Reid, a long-serving political worker for the CP, notably in the Organisation Department, who knew all of Central's MDs. Immediately after his appointment, the Board discussed detailed proposals for reducing the staff from what appears to be an astonishingly high level of fifty. 'Further it was agreed that the maximum wage should be £6.10.0, and that the Manager should reduce wages in excess of this amount by stages as can be agreed with the employees concerned'. The staff was reduced to 28 in November, later to 25, and by September 1948 there were 20 people employed. Among other measures taken to ease the financial situation were the letting of rooms to other organisations – at various times the Co-operative Arts Service, the London Trades Council, Progressive Tours, and the International Brigades Association had rooms in Parton Street. Stock worth £2,400 in retail value was written off – largely because it was out of date with the end of the war. Proposals were discussed for improving magazine terms; presumably Challenge (the Young Communist League paper) did not agree, as they took over their own distribution temporarily.

In September, the Report of Directors to Shareholders at

the AGM stated: 'The turnover in 1945 increased by £13,500 on that of 1944 but this was to some extent due to the increased political activity due to the General Election in May. During the last half of 1945 new conditions arising out of the ending of the war became apparent. Sales of political literature were seriously affected by the new situation and particularly by the development of the campaign against the Soviet Union'. The impact of the political situation, the growing anti-Communism of the Cold War, on Central Books was quite clear; in May 1947 a report blamed the decline in turnover on the 'slump in sales of political lines and the elimination of the wholesale trade in the general lines in the latter part of 1946'.

There are two curious entries in the minutes at the end of 1947 relating to staff: first, there was a 'Proposal to reduce the Staff Doctor to half the present time' and there was even a counter proposal to dispense with the job completely. This was the 'Party' doctor who worked at King Street and other CP enterprises: presumably each business had to pay part of his wages. The second relates to the first in a series of thefts that have dogged the company over the years, though whether this was more or less than other companies or other radical organisations is open to speculation: 'The Manager reported that the Accountant had absconded on November 10 and as result of subsequent investigations defalcations to the extent of £289.17.8 were discovered'. It was agreed to prosecute, and the offender was convicted the following month.

1948 saw no easing of the financial situation – it was noted that risk of bad debts had considerably increased in India and the Middle East. District bookshops were having problems: 'It was agreed that the Southampton Bookshop be written to on their failure to observe the agreement for reducing their outstanding account'. District bookshops were periodically 'on stop'. A lot of time at Board meetings was spent discussing the Liverpool shop and to a lesser extent the one in Chatham; in May 1950 the Liverpool shop was closed and the stock taken over by the Merseyside Area Committee of the CP who were granted a loan of £50, interest-free for two years, to help them pay for the stock. The Huxsteps complained that Central and the Party should find alternative work for them when they were replaced; Central did not agree, but all the same offered him a job in the Accounts Department in London and tried to find a job for his wife. To jump ahead slightly, in 1952 there were strains in the Accounts Dept and it was felt Dan Huxstep could not keep up with the work; a letter was written to Mick Bennett, the CP representative on Central's Board, asking if he could be found 'a caretaker or doorkeeper type of job or a simple clerical job... as the Company's financial position makes it impossible for us to carry passengers. We feel it is impossible to sack him... he will be over 70, has a wife and two children and no prospect of getting another job'.

1948 and 1949 saw repeated debates and arguments with Thames Books (the chain of small bookshops belonging to the CP's London District – there were eight of them in 1946) over slow payment and terms of discount, plus disputes over orders from the London branches. Despite these entries in the minutes, and despite Central Books' name and despite the image of a dominating centralism in the Communist movement, Central ultimately had no say in how local bookshops were managed – they were each the responsibility of their own District. However, these shops often made appeals for assistance from Central Books, especially with extended credit, but also for advice on trade and administrative problems, legal problems etc. Central went out of its way to service the bookshops, sometimes excessively so, and this led to a bit of a dependency culture to the extent that shops would order single copies of books, or even large quantities, from Central instead of opening accounts with publishers directly, or using wholesalers as they should have done. None had the resources of Central and usually they relied on voluntary help, the quality of which could vary enormously. Generally these shops were a bit dull and predictable in their content and their displays. However, Arnold Rattenbury, the poet, who was the Party's Propaganda Secretary in the West of England and thus responsible for the bookshops, remembers one in 1951 that was a bit different: 'I remember on my first visit that the shop window carried a washing line with, pegged to it, pamphlets by Marie Stopes, Harry Pollitt, an introduction to the *Karma Sutra* and something advocating variety in sexual position… we closed it in a fit of puritanical horror'.

In 1945, there had been 32 Party shops outside London, in such unlikely centres of revolutionary activity as Stroud, King's Lynn, Cheltenham, Wrexham, and Caerphilly; they were often called The People's Bookshop, or Progressive Books and there were also a couple of Modern Bookshops. By 1967, there were 18, but eight of these were literature depots in CP offices. The CP, and sometimes Central Books, would organise occasional conferences on Party literature sales and these took up a lot of resources; the Board spent a lot of time discussing the bookshops – even in 1980, by which time there were far fewer of them, there was a monthly report of sales and debts. Financial problems were discussed with regularity throughout the late 1940s and into the 1950s. In July 1948 two new problems emerged: a big increase in wholesale stock (it's not clear when wholesaling started again) and an increase in export debts. Turnover had dropped from £100,000 in 1945 to £75,000 in 1946 and then sales remained around £55,000 on average for the mid 1950s, dropping to £47,000 in 1959 before climbing steadily in the 1960s. Wage demands were recurrent: in September 'a demand for increased wages from members of the Despatch Department was examined. It was decided that the Wage Rates should continue to be based on the Union Rates'.

A surviving piece of correspondence from 1952 hints at the stresses of this period; the chairman, Robin Page Arnot, was writing to Gladys Percival, congratulating her on ten years service: 'We know that in the course of these ten years you have often had to work under great difficulties, had to take responsibility for a number of different departments in turn and on occasions even had to carry the main burden. But whatever the problems and trying circumstances, we have never looked to you in vain; you never refused to undertake difficult tasks and step into the breach when a crisis made this necessary'. Gladys replied: 'Please accept and convey to the directors my very warm thanks for the pen given to me on my tenth anniversary at Central Books. I hope I shall be able to put the pen to good use both for Central Books and the Movement'.

News was not all bad: in December 1948 the Board 'accepted the estimate from the builders for War Damage Repairs on the Parton Street building':it is not known how much this was, but it must have been helpful. There was a celebratory note soon after this: in August 1949 'In view of the 10th anniversary it was agreed to approve the grant of about £10 towards the cost of the annual staff party, and also to make a small presentation to the original directors who are still members of the Board and to those members of staff who have been with the Company throughout this period'.

A formal decision was announced in December 'that members of staff who are parliamentary candidates at the General Election be entitled to leave without pay from the date of dissolution to polling day', though presumably those who were not candidates weren't too happy at the extra work involved.

the 1950s

This decade did not start out well – in January 1950 an alleged libel in one of the magazines Central distributed, *Free Bulgaria*, led to the threat of legal proceedings. This was a potential problem for all distributors, but even more so for a distributor of political material; lawyers would read the imported journals from Eastern Europe and some copies were never distributed, but some articles did slip through. In this case, the minutes do not record the outcome. (The most serious legal case turned out to be one against the anti-fascist magazine, *Searchlight*, in the 1990s, which did cost us some money). 1951 saw another senior member of staff suspended 'for systematic infringement of the Company's regulations as to the handling of cash, daily payments into the bank etc.'.

In December 1952 Margaret Mynatt became MD. She was born in Austria; she worked in Berlin on a German CP newspaper, was close to Brecht's circle (actually inheriting some of the royalties from *The Threepenny Opera*) and she worked with Austrian refugees before the war. She worked for Reuters, and then went to the *Soviet Monitor*, which she managed with a large staff during the war. She has been described by Betty Reid as 'devoted, totally committed, conscientious', and by various people as slightly on the authoritarian side. Arthur Mendelsohn, the rep at this time (he had worked in Thames Books, and was later to be the manager of Collets International Shop), 'liked Margaret despite her dogmatism' and describes her as 'a woman of iron will, who suffered appalling health, but kept going notwithstanding'.

The 'non-arrival of *Stalin's Collected Works* affected sales figures' in March 1953. 1956 was looking like a good year. Trade invoices for the last quarter of 1955 were treble the same period in 1954 and Mail Order sales were also treble. A new 'Accounting Machine' costing £457 was purchased in May. In February it had been agreed to look for bigger premises as there was so much work, but the company was overtaken by events because, in June, the company received the first notification from the council that Parton Street was to be re-developed. (Parton Street ran at an angle from Red Lion Square into Southampton Row; it doesn't exist today). Perhaps this was seen as a good sign – at the same meeting the Board gave a bonus (totalling £250 in all) to be split among all who had worked at Central for one year or more – 'the staff had been very gratified and asked the Manager to express their appreciation to the Board'.

But events in the outside world were to affect Central Books. First, the Suez crisis hit foreign sales – 'it was agreed to give extended credit in view of the delay of deliveries' in December. Then there was the Hungarian uprising and its political fallout, which decimated CP membership and had a disastrous effect on Central Books, as literature sales slumped and bookshops, which had had enough difficulty trying to survive in the Cold War atmosphere, declined even further. In February 1957 the manager reported a 'steep decline in sales to District Bookshops (mainly London & Home Counties)' and in August 'a very serious position': there was a decline in sales (due to political events and Lawrence and Wishart publishing fewer titles); a breakdown of arrangement on imports from the USSR between CB, Mezhdunarodnaya Kniga (literally 'International Books', this was the Soviet organisation that dealt with the import and export of books) and Collets; the virtual end of orders from China; increased overheads from the new premises which also tied up cash; and on top of this there were trading losses.

All these events had rather overshadowed the short, but important, move of the warehouse to 37 Grays Inn Road on 22 February 1957. This address was to serve as the registered office for several of the CP's companies – Rodell Properties, Caledonian Press, Farleigh Press. All moves are expensive, and this was no exception: premises, fixtures and fittings at Grays Inn Road cost £3,325; repairs £650; removal £100; shelves £450; a goods lift was to be installed later (it never was). 'In the meantime, a small shop was to be opened at the end of April', but owing to staff shortages the shop was unable to open as planned – it was to open two years later.

The new building was not suitable for warehousing: it was really a largish town house (as Parton Street had been) transformed into offices above a shop; the rooms, reached by narrow winding stairs, were very small. Despite this, working life at Central was in many ways like that at any other distributor: there were the same tasks of invoicing, picking and packing, posting, delivering (at times Central used its own van in London, at others this was contracted out). Customers had to be chased for payment; there were always problems of space as new books arrived, and there were negotiations over terms.

But, in the early decades, the books and magazines that were distributed, and the customers supplied, were distinctly out of the ordinary. The magazines, a part of the business that gave CB an unusual profile and that played a crucial role in our expansion as we shall see, were divided between those from the socialist countries and home-grown Communist journals. The former, heavily subsidised and cheap, glorified the heroic achievements of the Soviet Union, GDR or China in glossy images (*Soviet Woman, GDR Review, China Reconstructs*); sales were considerable within Party organisations, even up to about 1975 (though they were declining). The CP magazines were of varying interest: the internal weekly/fortnightly *World News/ Comment/Focus* had little interest to those outside the CP – and tended to be a bit dry and overly serious, though they were not without controversies, especially during pre-Congress discussion time (the CP was often more like a collection of various parties and pressure groups rather than a monolithic organisation). *Marxism Today*, which started in 1957, also had its share of controversies even before the better known period under Martin Jacques in the 1980s, though it, too, was very serious in its theoretical debates. In between there were dozens of different special interest papers (*Woman Today*, *Challenge*, *Architects & Allied Technicians Group Bulletin*, *Medicine in Society*, *Realism*, *Esperanto Group Bulletin*, *Economic Bulletin*, *Our History*, *Music and Life*, *Red Letters*, *EuroRed*, *Education Today & Tomorrow*, *Jewish Clarion*, *Africa Newsletter*, *Labour Monthly*, *World Marxist Review*, *Science Bulletin*), plus papers from other left groups (*Young Socialist*, *Irish Democrat*, *Labour Research*).

The Communist movement published an enormous amount of material; this was disseminated from Central Books to the Party Bookshops or District literature depots, from where it would be sent on to branches, and each branch had – or was exhorted to appoint – a 'literature secretary' who often visited every branch member to supply them with their choice of journals and pamphlets. For a forthcoming bibliography, I have traced over 1,500 pamphlets published by the CP at national level (plus nearly 900 by Districts and branches). Print runs would generally vary from 1,000 for the more specialist titles to 10,000, 50,000 and even 100,000 at the CP's peak. Several times a year there would be a major pamphlet by a leading Party figure, or one on an industrial theme, and these especially were heavily promoted. There was a sense of obligation to sell as many copies as possible, whatever the quality, and Central would be involved in helping set targets for Districts, checking on these targets, distributing the material and then chasing payment from the Districts and shops. Inevitably, not everything sent out or purchased by members was sold or read: the comedian Alexei Sayle tells a story of his bed resting on unsold copies of the *Daily Worker*, that his Communist parents had not got round to selling. Still, it would be interesting to know if any other political, religious, or cultural organisation gave such emphasis to education and self-education in this period. Of course, this tradition can be traced to the previous century, and is part of the socialist tradition in general, but it reached a particular height within the CP.

Monday was the day books and magazines were picked, and packed, at Central: they were then sent out to the Districts on Tuesday. Thursday was 'lit. day' in the shops and there would be a steady stream of 'lit. secs' collecting their quota, though many left it to Saturday. Glen Baker, who worked in the Despatch Department from 1973 to 1976, remembers Jack Eighteen, a dock worker who became the London District Literature Secretary, and a Board member of Central, coming into the Despatch department to collect material most days. There would be bookstalls at many meetings – again supplied from Central to the shops or collected from the warehouse – which could take a lot of time to prepare.

The whole distribution procedure was rather byzantine: Central sold its own order books to the Districts and Party shops (though only at a nominal cost!); invoices were on different coloured paper; and there was a special sale or return 'No.2 account' for shops – all encapsulated in a 12 page duplicated *Guide for Managers of District Bookshops and Literature Departments*. Even today Central produces its own returns sheets for shops to fill in when returning magazines. But perhaps most book warehouses of the period would have recognised something in our odd procedures – it is easy to forget how much paperwork was involved in a business, even 20 years ago.

An item appeared in the minutes of February 1956 that reflected a change in the booktrade: 'The Manager reported that more and more publishers were agreeing to pay postage and carriage to booksellers'. This is so accepted now that it will appear strange to many that once shops paid carriage. It was obviously a significant change for Central, financially; it was only in 1976 that the company finally paid all packing and postage charges on deliveries to CP shops, and it was estimated that this would cost 5% of total turnover, but it saved a lot of time as it meant an end to the complicated procedure of charging shops a percentage of carriage. References in the minutes to the 'normal' booktrade were few and far between, and it was only in 1977 that the first reference to the Booksellers' Association or Publishers' Association appeared. Such a high proportion of trade was with the Party shops, and later with other radical shops, that the general booktrade was perhaps somewhat irrelevant for a long time. This can be seen in figures from 1950: 70% of business was with the CP shops, 14% was export trade, 11% was retail and only 5% was trade and libraries. And even in 1980, excluding CP shops, other left/alternative shops accounted for close to half of the sales to our top 35 UK customers.

There were a couple of personnel changes in the late 1950s: Peter Wheeler, who had been both MD and Company secretary at different times, resigned over Hungary. In January the Board stood for a minute's silence in memory of Ben Bradley who had just died. He had been company secretary during the War and a director since then; he was one of the 'Meerut Prisoners' put on trial in India in 1931, after he and others had gone there to assist in setting up trade unions. The Board donated £25 to a fund to provide security for his young daughter. Some of the other CP representatives on the Board of Central were distinguished figures in the labour movement. Robin Page Arnot was a famous historian of the mining unions; Clemens Palme Dutt was a writer and historian; Peter Kerrigan was an influential industrial organiser for the CP; there were two future CP General Secretaries who were directors for a short time (John Gollan and Nina Temple).

The Board of Central Books was made up of a representative from the CP's Executive Committee, the MD and secretary of the company, the MD of Lawrence and Wishart, sometimes an accountant, and any co-opted members as thought useful. Robin Page Arnot was a director from 1939 to December 1977; Clemens Palme Dutt from 1939 to November 1967; Reuben Falber, a long-standing full-time worker for the CP and one time Assistant General Secretary, and for many years responsible for the Party businesses, served from February 1955 to December 1991 (over half the lifetime of both the CP and Central Books).

This is a suitable point to consider the relationship between Central and the CP. Contrary to most expectations, the CP did not interfere in the running of Central Books at all. On a few occasions, the CP was asked by the Board to help when the financial position was difficult. But money was never given by the Party: there were loans, for example from the *Daily Worker*, in 1956, and from Democratic Left, the successor organisation to the CP, in 1991; the CP bought the lease on Grays Inn Road in 1981 from Central and, in 1990, helped by paying three years advance rent for the CP Archives which were housed in Central's warehouse. But all these transactions were on a strictly business basis: there was interest on the loans and a charge on the building, and the purchase of the lease was a very astute move! There was no sentimentality shown, as we shall see when the shop came to be closed. Historians of the CP have not really looked at the considerable business acumen that was shown in business and property deals over the years. When Central's finances were on a sound footing, there would be a discreet request for a contribution to the election fund, and old reps' cars might be donated to the General Secretary, so in fact more money went out than came in. But this all involved small amounts – Central never made big profits.

But of course there was a political relationship. All the MDs were in the CP, and so were all department managers till about 1980, and most afterwards till the late 1980s.

The appointment of MDs was always ratified by the Central Organisation Committee, and the Political Committee would be informed. This latter committee was elected by the

Executive Committee, itself elected by Congress, to look after the running of the Party; there was a nominal representative of the Political Committee on the Board right up to the end of the CP's existence, but, with the exception of Reuben Falber, it was not seen as a priority for them and they often did not attend in later years. For instance, between 1980 and 1991, there were five different representatives, and one never attended at all. However, it must be said that with Reuben on the Board, there was no great need for anyone else, even after his retirement from the Executive Committee, such was the confidence in him. Reuben can only remember one occasion when the Political Committee discussed Central Books between 1955 and 1991, and that was when he himself presented an item for information. Iris Walker, however, had regular meetings with Nora Jeffrey and then Tony Chater, the heads of the CP's Press and Publicity Department (nominally responsible for Central Books as it had been for the Workers' Bookshop). She also attended reports from the Executive Committee for District Secretaries, held every two months, which were quite important meetings in the CP hierarchy.

Somebody from the Political Committee, or Central Organisation Committee, might get involved if there were serious personnel problems, or perhaps a dispute with Collets if this got serious. Betty Reid can remember giving reports from the Organisation Department to members of staff at Central. All the CP businesses were more or less autonomous. An interesting example of this occurred in 1984, when Central's Board complained to the Political Committee, in vain, about *Marxism Today* taking away its subscriptions from CB to a commercial firm.

Although there was a legal dispute with John Calder (his Skyline Press was distributed by CB at 6% of invoice value, which seems an impossibly low rate now!), the 1950s ended on a positive note. The company was looking for larger premises for the shop: Lambs Conduit Street was considered but rejected. It's interesting that all the premises from the

1930s till 1977 were in a half mile radius in the Clerkenwell area. In April 1959 the Parton Street shop closed. The official opening of the Grays Inn Road shop was on 14 April by John Berger – who arrived with a leg in plaster due to a recent motor bike accident. £30 was spent on refreshments; several local MPs were present and the event was reported in trade and local papers.

always on the march for peace and socialism

always a splendid selection of progressive books and magazines to be found at

CENTRAL BOOKS

| order by post | come and browse |

| write for free catalogue |

find everything you want to read at

CENTRAL BOOKS
37 Grays Inn Road London WCI

F.P. Ltd. (T.U.), Aldenham, Herts.

An interesting publicity leaflet, with an attractive drawing. Note the variety of typography and the language. 'Peace and socialism', 'march', 'progressive' were typical of communist vocabulary, even the use of 'always' emphasises the certainty of the inevitable future victory as long as enough effort is put in.

The first set of minutes of the 1960s report a dispute with Lawrence and Wishart: 'The Manager reported that the question of excess deliveries had been taken up at the L&W Board meeting which had been informed that in future we would be unable to accept books except in quantities agreed beforehand'. From 1946 to quite recently the MDs of both companies were members of each other's Boards (L&W decided in the early 1990s not to have a rep from Central). Diana Poulton, on our Board from 1946 to 1949, was a distinguished flautist and musicologist. Betty Reid recalls her as being 'very pleasant—a bit fragile—not very political'. An unusual but very interesting figure in the panoply of CP businesses, apparently she got bored with her work at L&W – and presumably with Central Books' Board meetings as well. The subsequent managers of Lawrence & Wishart were Maurice Cornforth till 1977, Jeff Skelley till 1987, and since then Sally Davison, who is still on our Board. Occasionally disputes arose such as this one; from Central's point of view, excessive stock levels and unannounced deliveries were the major problem – though with a fair number of L&W's books being printed in the Soviet Union at that time (sometimes a L&W title page would be inserted in an edition printed there) this was an unavoidable hazard; another problem would be late publication dates but this affects all publishers. From L&W's side, errors in stock figures and loss of stock were the most common complaint (but any publisher or distributor reading this will know that this is endemic to warehouses!). There was a more serious dispute in the mid-1970s after Central had inadvertently charged L&W too much for postage, but it was settled after strong representations from L&W.

It was not just books from the Soviet Union that could cause problems; late in 1960 the minutes record ' – the arrival (unordered) of 6,000 volumes of selected writings by Lenin from China; agreed we could not handle them'. It's not clear whether they were returned, passed on to someone else, or a compromise was reached.

Storage was a permanent problem for Central – both Parton Street and Grays Inn Road were inappropriate for warehouse use. Some of the sites used for storage have already been mentioned, and in October 1960 the company again rented space at the Marx Memorial Library in Clerkenwell Green, at the cost of £475 p.a. It was planned to move the Despatch Department there, but this decision was then reversed. A basement in Farringdon Road was considered, but this was not taken up 'because of rodents'. Other sites that were rented for storage for various periods included: Lambs Conduit Street, Northington Street (off Grays Inn Road), Coram Street and the *Daily Worker* premises in Farringdon Road. Space there (on the 5th floor!) was rented in October 1973; it was full by January 1974 and vacated in July 1975 – then space in Wapping was rented from Merlin Press. In 1976, storage at Wapping and Clerkenwell Green was costing £2,600 p.a. A lot of time must have been spent looking at premises and negotiating terms, let alone moving stock around, as also happened in a later period of expansion in the 1990s. Other problems could arise in these temporary storage spaces: in 1969 the minutes note that 'As a result of carelessness, a basement at Clerkenwell Green had been flooded – stocks to a retail value of c£1,000 had been damaged. The builders admitted liability and the matter is now being pursued'. Perhaps this was a blessing in disguise – some of the old stock was unsaleable, and the insurance money would have been more useful. On the subject of premises, it was only in 1961 that final settlement was received from the London County Council for the redevelopment of Parton Street – in total the amount was £3,500.

Some of the problems associated with the distribution of Soviet books have been referred to. As trade with the Socialist countries was an important part of the business – together with staff relations, and premises, the subject dominates the Board minutes – it's worth looking in some detail at what this involved. There were times when this provided a crucial income for Central, but there were others when it was a burden in terms of space in the warehouses, in terms of time spent negotiating, and even in financial terms. Storage was a problem for Central, but also for the Soviet publishers: warehouses for foreign language books were not high on the priority for rebuilding in the USSR after the war; planning was cumbersome and print runs of books were based on false expectations; on one occasion – with the *Marx and Engels Collected Works* - L&W might have given inflated predictions in order to ensure the project went ahead, but usually it was the Soviets who got quantities wrong. Mezhdunarodnaya Kniga were so keen to get Central to take large numbers of books, that Central was able to get them to agree to send 20% on firm sale, and 80% on consignment that would only be paid for when sold. When Iris Walker was manager, later in the sixties, she went on average every other year to the USSR. One of the characters she had to negotiate with as head of Progress Publishers had been Stalin's last secretary. At least one of the MK staff in London was probably engaged in other 'activities': one had an appointment at Grays Inn Road one day, but was not able to attend as he was expelled by the British government that very day, in one of those periodic tit-for-tat series of expulsions; several MDs noted that some of their Russian negotiators knew very little about the book trade!

On the positive side, MK paid in advance for subscriptions for magazines (and they paid more than the trading companies of the other Socialist countries) and these subscriptions were at one time about 25% of our business. The Subscription Department and Commission Export were an important part of Central Books till the move to Wallis Road in 1990, by which time there was only one person working on this. Frank Scardifield ran this department, till he retired in 1986, with great efficiency and huge amounts of paperwork (the Soviets had to be provided with some documents in nine copies); at its height, there were four people in this department quite isolated from the rest of the company in the attic of Grays Inn Road. Also on the positive side, Soviet books were cheap and profit margins high – if they could be sold. Occasionally, there were some genuinely good sellers: Mayakovsky, some war reminiscences, art books, and Bilibin's beautifully illustrated children's books which were so successful that Collets tried to obtain the contract for importing them. The Soviets also paid annually for promotions, storage (after much negotiating), and repping. In fact, this helped finance one rep, but as he was unable to get orders for the books, in many cases he just gave up showing them to the book trade.

This was the downside: the books were just not geared to the Western book trade. Despite numerous visits to and from Moscow, MK could not understand why, if they printed and sold out of hundreds of thousands of copies of a book in their country, CB could not sell a few hundred in the UK. Often the translations were not up to scratch, the production values were very different, but the main reason was the content – only with Perestroika was there some understanding of this, and an attempt to adapt, but it was too late by then. On the rare occasion when there was a book with really good sales potential, it might turn out that they could not reprint it, as the quota of paper had been taken up for the next few years. Or they might seek to sell more marketable books through other companies: they produced a good chess book that they planned to sell to Batsford, till they were told it contravened the agreement with Central. On another occasion, Central arranged a sale of General Zhukhov's wartime memoirs to a book club, only to find MK could not supply the agreed quantity, leaving CB liable for a claim for compensation. In Iris Walker's time, Central persuaded W H Smith to take the magazine *Sputnik* – then MK wanted to supply direct instead of going through Central – MK ended up giving CB compensation for the loss of trade.

There were many technical books published in the USSR, but those distributed by Central had very low sales (Robert Maxwell used his knowledge of Russian, and his financial clout, to get the most interesting manuscripts for Pergamon Press, his technical publishing company).There were numerous arguments over stock levels – it was almost impossible to get their agreement to dump books, and remaindering was usually out of the question (though some of their books can be seen in remainder shops to this day: unfortunately they did not sell even when reduced).

Orders from the USSR could fluctuate dramatically from one year to the next: 'There was an expected drop in orders from MK this year (1964) to £3,000 from £15,000 in 1963 and £20,000 in 1962: due to reductions in allocation of foreign currency for book purchase'.

To sum up, relations with the Soviets were not governed by normal market relations. Their over-centralised economy was cumbersome and inflexible; they did not understand the UK trading environment, and political decisions took precedence over market conditions in deciding what and when to publish.

Slow payments from China, Hungary and Cuba all caused cash flow problems at various times: it was not unknown for CB to suspend supplies because of this. Not all decisions regarding trade with Eastern Europe were unanimous: in August 1965 Reuben Falber wanted his disagreement minuted over the decision to send the MD to Hungary: he said it was more important to concentrate on the home market, while two years later, Iris Walker wanted her disagreement noted over the terms of proposed trade with Cartimex of Rumania.

For two decades, one of the greatest problems faced by the company was a shortage of appropriate staff – or even, quite simply, of staff . The minutes show that the matter was first raised in March 1961: 'The Manager reported on the serious staff shortage and the almost insoluble problems connected with finding suitable replacements', and it was only in 1980 that it disappears from the Manager's report. Over that period, various measures were taken but the minutes are regularly full of almost desperate reports: 'Staff shortages: one Despatch worker left without giving notice, two Periodicals Department staff left including the manager' (Nov. 1961); 'impossible to find a suitable candidate to take charge of the Periodicals Department on Mrs Curran's departure' (Jan. 1962); 'Sales could have been greater had there been the staff to deal with accumulated orders' (Aug. 1964); 'Unable to replace Mrs Bolgar in Accounts Department; Mrs Clark offered to return if CB bought her a bicycle to facilitate her journey to and from Crawley station where she lived – agreed.' (May 1965). In January 1966 an accounts machine operator was taken on from an agency at £20 per week – this was after the accountant threatened to resign due to overwork. 'The Manager reported that due to increasing part-time staff it was becoming impossible to conduct consistent work, particularly in the Sales Department' And the problem continued into the 1970s: 'the serious staff problem... had further deteriorated in that the Van Driver and a Clerk in the Periodicals Department had decided to return to the provinces because of accommodation difficulties'; and a final example from October 1974: 'Due to illness/short staffing, CB was operating with staff of 9 instead of 20'. Shortage of staff actually led to the shop closing on Saturday mornings for a while. A personnel problem of a rather different nature occurred around this period: the van was found abandoned, and it turned out that the driver had been on drugs – the manager retrieved the driver from hospital.

Managers often showed great flexibility in fulfilling several roles simultaneously, for instance if a Sales Manager or Accounts Manager had not been appointed. Central Books at this time was not a normal business in its staffing policies. Political considerations, rather than business skills, were crucial in appointments of senior managers (though if they could be combined so much the better!); many young comrades worked in Despatch before going to university, so there was quite a turnover of staff; wages were linked to those for CP full-time workers which were notoriously low (though CB always paid at least the going union rates). Activists and relatives of activists might be taken on regardless of suitability – the MD would get a phone-call from a leading member asking if a job could be made available. Wolfie Kodesh was a South African comrade who had sheltered Nelson Mandela at one stage before being expelled from the country; Jack Woddis of the International Department rang the MD, and Wolfie was found a job in the Periodicals Department. Other comrades who had retired from full-time Party work, or who had been sacked from their mainstream jobs for their political activity, were also given jobs; this was admirable from an internationalist and caring point of view, and many became excellent members of staff, but it was unorthodox practice for a business. The tendency was not to always advertise jobs, but to put the word out, or simply ask Party members whom it was thought might be appropriate (Glen Baker was asked by the General Secretary, in 1973, to work in the Despatch Department), or to appoint comrades who asked for a job (as happened in my case in 1986). This would, rightly, be frowned upon now as contrary to equal opportunities, and is not our practice.

Because there was a minimal pension scheme for CP workers, and none for Central Books' workers till the 1990s, staff often carried on working into their sixties, seventies and even eighties – again, fine for those who wanted and were able to do this, but it could cause some problems. There was a reluctance to ask people to leave, and there was certainly no standard retiring age, nor is there one today. In an era which undervalues and discriminates against older workers, this may be seen as a very positive approach, but it could reduce the amount of young blood entering the company. Several ex-members of staff commented during interviews that some of the old-timers in the past had got used to living on a comparatively low wage, could not get other work (sometimes for political reasons as well as age) and possibly got into a rut.

These comments may appear a bit negative, because there is also no doubt that there were many excellent members of staff who not only stayed a long time at the company but who were very skilled at their job and who could have undoubtedly got higher paid jobs in a more mainstream company, and this applies to packers, office staff and managers. Some people did indeed move on to very successful careers elsewhere within the book trade.

Some notable examples of long service were Mrs Scott the cleaner (18 years), Gladys Percival (1943–1973), Ulli Harris, Sales Manager, (1952–68), Frank Scardifield (1958–1986), Bill Allen (1956–1976), Judith Todd (1957–1981), and some of the Directors who have already been mentioned. Robin Page Arnot must have been well into his seventies when the Board decided 'To assist Mr Page Arnot to avoid the rush hours on public transport it was agreed that he should take taxis at the company's expense'. In the early years of the company, there were regular presentations to members of staff for long service and on notable birthdays. This practice may appear rather quaint now, but was not uncommon in businesses several decades ago. Perhaps it makes Central appear a bit like a family firm, with a paternalistic board of Directors, and which was owned by an unseen, benevolent uncle based in King Street. It is certainly doubtful if many firms would have kept on someone like Joe Marks as long as Central Books did

(1962 – 1978) after the following Board minute from March 1963: 'The traveller, Joe Marks, had failed his driving test for the fourth time. It was agreed to sell the car and to purchase another one if and when J Marks passed his test'. As if this was not bad enough, two years later it was reported that 'The insurance company refused to provide comprehensive cover while J Marks was driving'. Joe is remembered with affection by all who knew him; I remember him repping – he was in his late sixties – when he visited Progressive Books in Liverpool in the late 1970s, with his huge brief cases; he used public transport then, so his unfortunate relationship with the car must have dogged him all his life. (A later rep turned out to have only a provisional licence so had to drive a three-wheeler for a year!).

A rather touching item appears in the minutes of September 1968 relating to age: 'Mr W Allen had reached the age of 65 and had asked the Manager if we now wished him to retire to make way for a younger person. He hoped to continue working until the age of 70, but did not wish to be a burden to CB during this period. It was agreed that the Manager should write a letter of appreciation for the comradely way in which he had raised the matter and to say that we look forward to his continued service with CB. It was also agreed to make a small token on the occasion of this special birthday'. Similarly, in April 1963 'The Manager raised the question of D Huxstep who was now over 80 years old and beginning to be somewhat forgetful. It was agreed to look into the question of retiring him either on a small pension or a payment of a lump sum'. This is the same man who appeared earlier in the story when he was also a subject of concern. In fact, Dan Huxstep was just transferred from Accounts to Periodicals! He stayed with the company till, very ill, he finally retired in June 1974, aged 91, writing to the Manager: 'I think I should like to retire altogether now – I hope this does not make a serious exageration (sic)of your problems of staffing and that the department will be able to cope. I shall treasure memories of CB and all the kindnesses that I have received from yourself and the staff'. Sadly, he died the following month.

A job at Central was not viewed like other jobs – staff were 'doing a job for the movement' and though they might be paid accordingly, i.e. very poorly, there was a real sense of commitment. Wage differentials were minimal. Figures from negotiations in 1978 provide an insight into wage differentials and comparisons with CP staff, who were slightly higher paid then:

> CB MD £57.50 – CP Political Committee member: £58.02
> Managers £55.00 – Political Workers £57.25
> Staff £52.00 – Technical Workers £56.00

It is interesting to note that differentials had decreased since 1951, when the MD got 12% more than other managers, and 30% more than the basic wage.

Managers were just as likely to have been active in the CP – and not just card-carrying members – as any staff member; this is certainly true of all MDs from Margaret Mynatt onwards. They may also have had responsibilities in other labour movement organisations. And generally the same was true of Directors. To take just one example: James Gray, who was company secretary from 1945 till his death in 1951, was a member of the Institute of Chartered Accountants of Scotland and he was also active in the Clerical and Administrative Workers' Union.

There are some amusing and telling incidents recorded in the minutes which show how the highly developed political culture was accepted as the norm by everyone in the company. In May 1960 the manager reported with some pride that 'the Central Books van participated in the May Day march and the Aldermaston march'. In October 1963 the Directors 'agreed that Iris Walker could have time off to work in by-election – as long as her wages were refunded and it was not to be repeated' (obviously finance was an issue then). In September 1974 the Board meeting was cancelled because the majority of members were involved in the General Election – and this was not the only occasion this occurred. In April 1969 'At a Staff Meeting certain members of the staff had raised the question of closing the business on 1st May, but it was agreed that those who wished might have time off for the purpose of attending a demonstration' – and pay was not deducted.

Up to the early 1970s, all CB staff would be in the CP, or extremely close; with the decreasing membership of the Party, and with a more open political approach, non CP members were employed regularly after that. Generally most were left wing, and there was a sprinkling of anarchists, Greens and even Trotskyists in later years. Many put in extra hours of unpaid work at bookstalls at political events, as well as on the premises. Many former members of staff recall the camaraderie with affection – even when they were not members of the CP, and possibly even critical of it, like Dave Rosenberg, a Trotskyist-leaning van driver in the early 1980s; Dave describes his two stints of work at Central as some of the most enjoyable periods of his working life (he saw his work as 'literally spreading the word'). He appreciated the relative autonomy of his job and the political discussions with fellow warehouse staff.

But things were not all rosy: Dave describes a 'harsher regime – high turnover and bad atmosphere' when the financial situation deteriorated, and is critical of the lack of involvement of staff in decision-making and the remoteness of the Board. There are more references in the Minutes to Staff meetings and representations to the board in the 1970s. Conflicts developed between union and management – not helped by the fact that everybody was in the same union branch! This membership of the same USDAW branch continued till very recently when managers joined a different section of the union. Another curiosity of life at Central was the tradition of the closed shop: every new member of staff had to join the union – nothing remarkable about this in a Communist Party business, but when the closed shop became illegal under Thatcher, Central's management still insisted that everybody join the union. If the 1980s and 1990s saw a more businesslike approach, the union also became more 'normal' and management, though still nominally entitled to attend meetings, stayed away.

Disputes did occur. One dispute went to ACAS as we shall see, and a couple went to Industrial Tribunals before being withdrawn at the last minute, but there are no records of strikes (Collets had a famous one in 1988). Working hours were very generous: a 35 hour week was instituted in May 1962 (a strange decision given the problems of staff shortages, but this measure was probably compensation for a low wage increase); the 34 hour week was 'won' in 1986. Maternity and paternity leave were much better than average. Wages were the main concern, and, in the early 1980s, there was a problem with redundancies, due to the financial crisis. It's probably fair to say that for a long time, management, including the Board, seemed remote from most staff and in some cases difficult to approach. The attempts by both sides to come to some consensus on staff involvement are evident from the Minutes (especially from 1986), but there was undoubtedly some suspicion on both sides.

There was a fairly serious breakdown in staff confidence in the management at one time; Glen Baker recalls that at the end of 1974 most Communist Party members signed a letter to the Directors, complaining that workers' views were not being taken into account and that decision making was autocratic. This complaint did not go through the Union: the letter was specifically written with reference to the CP constitution (and for this reason could not be signed by non-members, of whom there were some by this time). In particular, it referred to a clause which stated that it was the duty of members to raise matters detrimental to the Party's interests; the claim was that management behaviour was indeed detrimental. Reuben Falber, as usual, dealt with this episode and apparently dealt with it well; his task was made easier by the fact that one request in the letter naively said that as the signatories to the letter often took part in Party activity after work, they should be allowed to start work late! But the main content of the letter was treated seriously and raised at the Board; in January 1975 'A number of questions concerning Staff were discussed and proposals were made and approved, with a view to improving communications'. But it is not clear from the minutes what they were. A revealing sideline on this incident is that the CP members who did not sign – they either refused, or more probably were not asked – were the long-standing, older members who were perceived as having an excessive loyalty to management.

Turnover was averaging £150,000 in the late 1960s and early 1970s; the company was roughly breaking even, but financial crises occurred with depressing regularity at this time: 'Increase in overheads and an end to Cuban purchases led to a precarious position' (orders from Cuba had proved short lived): the number of staff was reduced (May 1965) – and this was not long after the big drop in trade with the Soviet Union. In May 1969 'It was agreed that everything possible was being done to maintain sales, and we could not offer any prospect of an improvement at the present time'. Still, the white heat of the technological revolution did reach the Dickensian premises of Grays Inn Road: the same Board meeting agreed 'to buy a new NCR machine in preparation for decimalisation'. In March 1973 'It was agreed that we purchase a new addressograph machine in place of the outdated machine at present being used. It was also agreed that we should purchase an electric typewriter providing a member of staff was prepared to use one'.

In February 1966, there was a Special Directors' Meeting. Margaret Mynatt insisted on retiring. The proposal was that Judith Todd would take over from April 1966, assisted by Iris Walker, with a view to the latter taking over at a later date. In fact, Judith Todd was never MD – though she might have 'held the fort' for a month till Iris took over in May. Judith, who was born in 1908 and who joined the CP in 1936, worked part-time at Central in the 1970s; she was also on the Board of Lawrence & Wishart. Betty Reid describes her as 'witty and erudite', and one of her lesser known skills was shown in the pseudonymous, satirical poems she wrote for the *Daily Worker*. She also acted as accountant for several of the CP businesses, working from an office in Grays Inn Road (she had to remove her filing cabinets which were still there when the shop was closed in 1992!). Judith was one of those professional Communist women who played an important background role in the CP businesses – Elspeth Munro was to fulfill a similar role from the early 1980s, providing Central with accounting and administrative expertise, though she was only on the Board for two years (and her files are still in the office).

Iris Walker, born in 1920, joined the CP in 1942 and immediately took an interest in literature sales in her branch of Saltley in Birmingham. On her release from essential war work in 1946, she started work in Key Books in Birmingham, and became manager in 1948 when she replaced Ernie Steele. Under her management, Key Books became probably the best Party shop outside London. Iris worked hard to build CP literature sales, organising pit-head and factory sales of pamphlets; she built up a library in the shop – until it was closed due to an increasing tendency for books not to be returned. She also organised poetry readings and 'meet the author' evenings. Her work in Birmingham led Peter Wheeler to invite her to attend the Board of Central Books. She left Birmingham in 1956 to live in Italy, but, on regular visits to England, she would work temporarily in Collets. Returning to live permanently in England in 1963, she was immediately asked to work for the Party again (Collets were annoyed they couldn't get her). She was put on the payroll of CB, but

**Iris Walker in Grays Inn Road.
The shop was long and narrow
and the shelves reached from
floor to ceiling, but it was
packed with books.**

worked in the CP's Press & Publicity Department, with a brief to extend literature sales. She would travel a lot, spending 4-6 weeks at any one time in the Districts.

When asked to become MD, Iris was initially very reluctant, feeling like most other MDs, that she was not qualified for the job; she tried, in vain, to persuade Margaret Mynatt to continue. There was an element of hostility to her as MD from a couple of people who had been intensely loyal to Margaret.

Today, in 1999, almost eighty, Iris is still selling books – at events organised by the International Brigades Association.

the mid-1970s to mid-1980s

The next Managing Director was appointed in June 1976. Dave Wynn had previously worked in the Research Department of the AUEW, the engineering union. Before he was appointed MD he had worked in all departments to get some experience of the company, but the staff had not been told of Iris Walker's pending retirement. He was of a new generation within the CP – young, dynamic, associated with the Eurocommunist wing of the Party, and not so interested in the Soviet connection (he hated dealing with MK!) – today he would be called a moderniser. He had no business experience or booktrade experience – his appointment was quite political in this sense, his brief being to rejuvenate the company. His comparatively short period saw the expansion of the company to new premises, a more modern management approach – attempts to improve management/staff relations, a more flexible wage structure and higher wages. His period as manager also coincided with an increase in left-wing publishing and bookselling that largely bypassed the CP, so it was difficult to find new publishers who would come to Central for distribution. Dave took over at the same time as a new, radical distributor was being set up: Publications Distribution Cooperative (or PDC); in July, Central sent an initial £25 donation to the fledgling organisation. Cooperatives were in the air in the radical booktrade, as in society in general, and the Communist Party was perceived as a bit old-fashioned or irrelevant. However, this was a time of change within the CP as well: a new edition of the Party's programme, *The British Road to Socialism*, was to appear in 1977, which finally laid to rest the idea of a British 'Revolution': the transformation of society was seen as a much more complex process; feminism was achieving some recognition, criticism of the USSR was more open. Organisationally, the Party was moving away from the traditional Leninist model. Although, with hindsight, these changes appear slow, overdue and timid, the CP was reflecting changes in society at large.

Items dealing with personnel matters are noticeably more positive in the minutes; the first board meeting after Dave Wynn's appointment 'Agreed to rationalise the wage structure raising the basic rate in Despatch and for telephonist/office worker to £40 per week'. Weekly meetings of department heads were instituted. 1977 saw the establishment of a Staff Committee. In 1978 it was minuted that, in case of maternity, the job will be held open for one year, and also that three days paternity leave would be granted; in 1979 it was 'agreed to look at the composition of the Board at the AGM and to seek ways for the staff to have more opportunity of meeting the Directors', though the outcome is not clear. December 1979 saw a 15% wage increase, plus an increment of £5 for those who had been with the company for five years or more.

In 1977 it was decided to seek new premises; premises were looked at in Upper Street, the company considered sharing with Lawrence & Wishart, and toyed with the idea of taking over Collets International Shop in Museum Street for its retail outlet, as they were moving to Charing Cross Road. But, in December 1977, CB signed a contract to rent, for £6,800 p.a., new premises at 14 The Leathermarket, near London Bridge. The Despatch Department moved in June the following year, and the office in October; the shop remained at Grays Inn Road and the upstairs offices were rented out.

The new premises were in a handsome early Victorian warehouse block (not surprisingly the old leather market)

A window display in Grays Inn Road to commemorate the Russian Revolution

surrounding a courtyard; access was through an archway intended for horses so some deliveries were difficult. There was a hazardous hoist system which involved staff strapping themselves in a harness and leaning out of the third floor before lifting parcels which had been loaded into a huge metal basket – there were never any injuries, though one day the hoist broke sending the basket crashing to the ground! Storage arrangements could now be ended in Clerkenwell and Wapping – for the first time all the stock was in one site. The office was the top one of four floors, and was open plan – a radical departure from the compartmentalised working environment of Grays Inn Road. In particular, the MD no longer had a separate room and this aided the development of a more open management. It marked a huge improvement in working conditions, especially for office staff.

The first new publisher for a long time was signed up for distribution, though International Publishers of New York (the publishing house of the American CP) had been handled since about 1963; this was Journeyman Press, set up by Peter Sinclair, who had once worked at Central (he was not the only ex-worker to become a publisher that CB distributed – Stephen Hayward, who had also worked at L&W as well as at Central, followed with Serif). Journeyman was not a big publisher, though they were very successful with an attractive series of reprints of some of Jack London's works, but taking them on must have made Central think about its contracts with potential publishers, about the possibility of expansion, and about the need to turn outwards for business. In this sense it was a sign of the future, even if a small one.

The retail shop was expanding greatly – in 1977 sales were up 23%, partly thanks to some huge bookstalls at labour movement events, but mainly at CP events such as the People's Jubilee at Alexandra Palace (£3,000) and the Communist University of London (£4,300). Communist Party membership may have been declining steadily, and there may have been splits in the Party from this period onwards (the New Communist Party broke away in 1977, the *Morning Star* from 1983), but there was a brief uplift of CP influence and activity associated with Eurocommunism, exemplified by the successful Communist Universities of London, and often identified later with the renewal of *Marxism Today*. This was partly reflected in the Party's publishing and distribution outlets and in the district bookshops, when the initiative was shown to take advantage of this intellectual renewal. This coincided with the rapid spread of radical bookshops from the mid 1970s to the mid 1980s (the intellectual and economic onslaught of Thatcherism was to deal a serious blow to this movement); feminist, gay, anarchist, independent and other political bookshops appeared apparently from nowhere (the generation of 1968 with a bit of capital?) and worked together in the Federation of Radical Booksellers; Collets were expanding; the Socialist Workers' Party flagship bookshop, Bookmarks, played the key role in organising the annual Socialist Bookfair which became a splendid non-sectarian event that had to be taken seriously by the whole booktrade – practically all the major academic publishers were represented with stalls, and discussion would often reveal strong left wing opinions by those behind these stalls.

This trend was seen not only in the retail trade, but in distribution (as well as PDC, there was Third World Distribution, based in Birmingham) and publishing - in fact the long term effects were more significant here. New left-wing and feminist publishers sprang up (Journeyman Press was at the smaller end of the spectrum: Virago and The Women's Press were much bigger), or expanded rapidly (Pluto and Verso). Many mainstream publishers started issuing radical books, sometimes in the form of whole new imprints, which previously were only available, generally speaking, from small publishers and in small radical shops.

There were still conflicts between companies in this golden age of radical co-operation; and the competition

Taking left books to the people

The Central Books triumvirate — (left to right) Jack Berlin, Bill Norris and Peggy Blatchford — in their newly expanded Holborn shop.

CENTRAL BOOKS is going places in 1980. And that includes to the Morning Star's "Beat the Tory Blues" festival at the Ally Pally on Sunday, June 15.

Thousands who may not have been to the bookshop at 37 Gray's Inn Road, London, WC1, will have Central Books come to them. Its stalls at the festival, displaying and selling a vast array of left books and periodicals, will be one of the main features of the giant multicultural event.

Bill Norris, who runs the shop with Peggy Blatchford and Jack Berlin, points out that only a staggeringly low percentage of people go into a bookshop regularly in the course of a year.

That is why it is increasingly the style of Central Books to go to people. And since the organisation has won a respected place on the left in British politics, each year it is putting on its book sales at more and more

trade union and labour movement occasions.

Central Books, founded after the last war to sell Communist Party and other left-wing literature, now supplies the libraries of 25 trade unions from the busy premises in Gray's Inn Road.

MAIL ORDER

There, Jack Berlin, ex-engineer and speaker of five languages, presides devotedly over the mail order department. He now sends his parcels to customers in 130 countries — the latest on the list being Zimbabwe.

The shop itself has just taken on a new and brighter look, with an expansion of 20 per cent in the shelf space.

There have been other changes since the shop was opened over 20 years ago. In the 1950s you wouldn't have seen

shelves devoted to such subjects as sexual politics, women's studies and community publishing.

And there is a far wider choice of periodicals among the 100 different titles on sale. You can get all the Communist Party publications (and it can be a surprise to see what a variety of them there are), along with Tribune, Socialist Worker, Gay News and many others.

"The shop used to be dominated by the Marxist classics," says Bill Norris. "We are far wider now, but we still sell at least one set of Lenin's Selected Works a month." And that means 46 volumes costing £158.

Whether that, or E. P. Thompson's latest essay, or a 10p "I didn't vote Tory" badge is your immediate need, a visit to the shop of Bill, Peggy and Jack is likely to be a fruitful and friendly experience.

An article from the *Morning Star*, dated 31 May 1980 with photo showing Jack Berlin, Bill Norris and Peg Blatchford in the shop

between Central Books and Collets, which can be seen as a minor leitmotif in this story, continued. In August 1976, the Board discussed the request by Collets to import Soviet English language books direct for the proposed new shop in Charing Cross Road; CB did not want to change the current contractual agreement, but did offer better terms. This was an example of the occasional scraps between the two companies for the better titles, and many hours were spent in negotiations. Collets was perceived as rather privileged compared to Central – bigger, better resourced, prime sites on Charing Cross Road, stronger links with the Socialist countries, ideal purpose-built warehouse in Wellingborough, etc. It even benefited from its looser ties to the CP, as sometimes the Soviets wanted a non Communist business link for some projects. Wages may have been slightly higher there, but there is evidence from several people who worked for both, that conditions and atmosphere were not as good at Collets as at Central. The shops in Charing Cross Road were an important outlet for CP and left-wing material, always being better known nationally, and internationally, than Central, which was the poorer member of the family on a poorer site. The frictions were not between the retail outlets, but between the managements of both companies over dividing up the spoils of imports and exports to the Soviet Union. The most profitable part of this business was the order for supplying subscriptions for magazines to Soviet institutions, and Collets had by far the major share of this; but most squabbles were over the importing of books from the Soviet Union, and especially the comparatively rare good-selling items like art books. In the end, though, Collets' expansion into the USSR and Eastern Europe did not do them any good; they may have got assistance to finance the grand International Shop in Charing Cross Road in the 1980s, but with the fall of the 'socialist' countries they lost too much of their trade to survive. Central had of necessity to concentrate on the home market, and adapt to the changing political environment well before this and as a consequence did survive.

Sales, which had been increasing in the couple of years before Dave Wynn started, passed from £300,000 to £500,000. So, at the end of his tenure, in 1980, sales were higher than ever before and the infrastructure at Central was better than ever before, but the company was not distributing enough publishers to finance it. CB had two buildings, was possibly overstaffed (this was certainly a break with recent tradition), the CP was entering a period of internecine struggle, and the economy was about to enter recession. Dave was a good delegator and one of his first decisions was to persuade Bill Norris (from the same Communist Party branch) to apply for a job in the shop, then appoint him manager of it a year later.

In September 1980, after Dave Wynn left (he stayed in the booktrade and had a very successful career with Oxford University Press), Alan Brooks was appointed Central's MD, largely on the recommendation of Jack Woddis of the CP's International Department. Alan was 40 years old, had previously worked for the Anti-Apartheid Movement, IDAF and the ANC. He had been educated in southern Africa; he joined the African Resistance Movement in South Africa, was imprisoned for two years and then deported to the UK. There were personnel problems, and combined with a difficult financial situation, this made things unpleasant for him. He was not at ease with the personnel side of the business and he did not enjoy the job. There was undoubtedly some political friction as well – he was not totally sympathetic to the direction the CP was heading in – but he was completely open about his politics, and Bill Norris' assessment is that any political differences that did exist were not as important as personal differences. Several of those interviewed talked of his great integrity, and his dislike of having to deal with hidden agendas and personal antagonisms – that sort of 'politics'. He came to the conclusion quite early on that the job was not right for him.

Wage negotiations which coincided with his arrival were difficult – the initial demand was for a 35% increase and it finally went to ACAS for arbitration, which awarded 15%. The same month that the wage negotiations were being reported, there is an unusually critical comment in the minutes: 'Performance of Despatch Department continues to be uneven, largely due to the inadequacy of the Manager. He and his colleagues have refused to implement a decision of the Management Cttee. to limit tea-breaks to 15 minutes (a.m.) and 10 minutes (p.m.)'. The minutes reflect a harsher tone, though it would be unfair to put this down solely to Alan; there is even a bitterness in one item that may just reflect bad minute taking: one member of staff 'called to account by the Management Cttee., declined to appear and indicated his intention to look for work elsewhere. Since then he has suffered a domestic calamity (fire gutted his flat); probably less keen now to change jobs'. He was dismissed for incompetence four months later.

The financial problems were serious. In July 1981, Alan estimated that a £50,000 injection was needed for the company to survive – this was when the sub-lease on Grays Inn Road was sold to the CP, to stave off financial disaster; at one stage during a Board meeting he floated the idea that on purely financial grounds, Central Books should close.

As has been seen already, periods that appear at first to be wholly negative often have positive elements, and this one is no exception. There were improvements in several areas. The stock position in the shop had got out of hand (Bill was the buyer who did not like to say no!), and this was dealt with. Both MK and L&W were persuaded to dump some very slow selling books, and remainder others. Wholesaling was looked at and the advantages reported on (at the beginning of 1981, there only seemed to be three titles sold on a wholesale basis). There was a hugely successful series of Soviet books – beautifully illustrated children's books by Bilibin – though this, together with the dreaded huge deliveries of the *Marx and Engels Collected Works* (known to all at Central as *MECW*), led to a recurrence of the old problem of storage. In February 1981 it was noted that '30 tons of *MECW* were moved to Farleigh Press (Watford); we had taken in nearly 11 tons of Bilibins'.

Sales of second hand books started in the shop, based on the remnants of James Klugmann's collection which were sold to raise money for the CP Library and Archive, after the more precious items had been passed on to various other institutions. 'Remnants' perhaps gives the wrong impression, as this was a huge collection which kept the second hand department going for years. James, a historian, had been the leading CP figure at Cambridge in the 1930s, the editor of *Marxism Today*, and a compulsive book-buyer: he built up one of the best labour history collections in the world, which he left to the Party. The first four weeks of selling these books brought in £1,500, a very useful sum at the time. There had been some small-scale selling of second hand books many years before: in 1947 the Board 'decided to approve trading in second hand Marxist classics' but it is not known how long this lasted.

The most significant development was the decision to buy a computer. This arose from a strategic review which was brought to the Board in May 1981. This suggested Central should:

a) seek substantial publisher lists to distribute
b) explore the possibility of financial investment in a microprocessor which was agreed to be essential for the modernisation of our systems, and which would free Sales Staff for more promotional and marketing activities and create a Sales force
c) avoid and reduce CB's activity in distributing individual titles/very small lists.

The other decisions may have borne fruit later, but the contract was signed for an Olivetti BCS3030 computer for £13,000 on a five year lease with an annual maintenance contract of £1,100. 'With a computer we would be able to make further cuts in staff' the manager reported: the decision was linked to trying to solve the financial crisis, it was not just a forward looking, positive decision to take the company forward with the benefits of new technology. It was estimated that two full-time and one part-time post would go within two months. There were long drawn out negotiations over the redundancies, with both sides making compromises and the union was thanked for its constructive approach. The computer arrived in March, but in November it was reported that 'progress was taking longer than anticipated due in part to mechanical failures'. (In November 1983 a second computer, an Olivetti 3030, was purchased for £5,000).

In February 1982, Alan Brooks resigned but he then agreed to work on till June. Reuben Falber would assume overall responsibility during the transition; the working directors and Elspeth Munro would handle management decisions. When interviewed, Reuben describes himself as 'not a particularly effective manager' but 'as holding the fort'.

...,for radical reading matter
Visit the shop or order by post
37 Grays Inn Road, London WC1
Open 9·30-5·30 Sats 10-2   01-242 6166

A humorous design used
on paper bags in the 1970s

However, Reuben had been involved with the company since 1955, was a decisive decision maker, had considerable business acumen and a lively mind and he took on some good publishers of books and magazines during his period. *The London Review of Books* and *Literary Review* were two of the magazines. One of the publishers Reuben worked with, even to the extent of organising financial assistance, was a company called Brilliance, a successful, but short lived, gay publisher.

While Reuben was always very supportive of managers, perhaps he seemed distant to some members of staff and he was involved in some confrontational personnel situations.

In July 1983 the Board discussed 'the difficulties of another distributor – agreed to examine carefully approaches from their suppliers'; this was Southern Distribution (PDC having split into two parts, with Scottish and Northern being based in Manchester); Reuben duly produced a careful report which looked at the problems of distributing small unprofitable publishers, of taking on national distribution of some of Southern's publishers which would cause difficulties for Scottish and Northern. Southern Distribution did go bankrupt and this led to an extension of Central's distribution project, starting with Sheba Feminist Publishers. In September it was agreed to seek national distribution for any publishers approaching the company; if this was not possible, then CB would accept supplying solely the south of England, but with the right to service orders from other parts of the country if they arrived unsolicited.

Comedia, who published a range of studies of radical businesses at this time, produced a comprehensive report for the Greater London Enterprise Board on Southern Distribution and its future, in the context of possible future grants. This report is an important document on the state of radical bookselling at the time; it commented on the range of alternative retailing and wholesaling, and its view of Central was very positive: 'In our view CB is now a relatively effective distribution service, operating on a sound financial basis which would be capable of expanding its services in a profitable manner'. This is one of the few outside assessments ever made of the company in its 60 year history.

Southern's demise did provide more opportunities, and greatly widened CB's publisher base; should the company have been more adventurous/ruthless and tried to get all the publishers who had been with Southern, and who eventually were to join the newly-established Turnaround Distribution? There was probably still some anti-CP hostility which would have hindered this. This period did establish Central as the leading magazine distributor (Turnaround took a decision not to handle magazines, as they were perceived as a major factor in Southern's failure). CB remains on friendly terms with Turnaround (one of their Directors worked at Central as a rep), even though there is the occasional overlap of interest, and occasional movement of publisher from one to the other. Is it a wild flight of the imagination to see these friendly relations between competing businesses as a remnant of that spirit of '68 already discussed above? Would two ordinary commercial companies act in the same way?

Bill Norris was appointed MD in 1984. Born in 1951, he joined the Communist Party in Cambridge as a student, after an early anarchist phase. The CP branch there was very large and active and several of his contemporaries turn up in the world of radical publishing, including Sally Davison, of L&W, to whom he had been married for a while. He travelled and did a few odd jobs before starting in the shop. Bill had overseen the expansion of the retail business – extending the area once the warehouse had moved, and extending the political range of the stock; more bookstalls were organised at outside events. By 1984, he felt he had done all he could there, and, in his words, was tiring of 'the feeling of being in a goldfish bowl': Grays Inn Road certainly did have large windows, but also as a small and unusual bookshop attracted some odd people at times! The appointment as MD was a bigger change than he had expected, and in his own words he 'didn't know what the job was at first' – there was never any question of management training at Central, people were thrown in at the deep end. Bill was to find great assistance at the Leathermarket from the dedication and business skills of Andrew Heywood – the company secretary for four years from 1984. Andrew's career took an unusual turn for an ex-Communist: he later ran a business belonging to the Duke and Duchess of Devonshire.

One of the earliest strategic decisions under Bill's management was to greatly reduce wholesaling, and then end it completely. For non-booktrade readers, the distinction between wholesaling and distribution may not be clear; the former meant Central picked certain titles, or occasionally a publisher's complete list, and ordered as required; a bookshop might order from the wholesaler to top up stock on titles quickly, usually in small quantity, or they might order from the publisher or their distributor directly. The distributor was the prime supplier for a publisher and held all their stock – and wholesalers would buy from them. Central got better terms on distribution than on wholesale. For CB, wholesaling originated as a help to its retail outlet, and to the CP bookshops up and down the country; it had developed in the 1980s as an apparently effortless way to achieve turnover; being based in London (where up to 50% of business might come from), and owning a van at the time, it could provide a rapid top-up service. It took some time to realise that there was a downside; all stock was firm sale, so CB shouldered the cost of unsold books; a lot of time was involved in administration, which should have been spent servicing the publishers distributed, as they were the core of the business; and, crucially, margins were tight. Other companies could provide a better wholesale service because they did nothing else, though CB specialised in academic and political books; the demise of the political shops did not help either.

Another early decision was to change computers. Arrangements were made and £25,000 was borrowed over five years from Rodell. The previous system was very basic, and was accounts based. There were only two screens so there was a problem of access, and people often stayed late to be able to use them. The computer did not affect most people (e.g. letters were still done on typewriters), and to enter books on the system one had to know the ISBN, so the procedure was cumbersome. The new system came from a company called Sweetens, initially with four screens; screens could be added, and more importantly, the software was developed to suit Central's needs over the years – it proved very flexible, but with weaknesses in accounts and word-processing; it was only replaced in 1999 by a PC based network from the same company, costing about £70,000. Computerisation in businesses is taken for granted as it is so common, but there are two implications worth reflecting on. Firstly, if the company had got it wrong over the timing, or the choice of system, the consequences could have been disastrous – many firms have failed because of errors in computerisation. Secondly, from a broader perspective, the longer serving members of staff have lived through a remarkable technological revolution, and have adapted from a paper and pen age to an electronic age – this is quite an achievement.

Bill also saw the need to broaden the range of publishers; it was still surprisingly difficult to get the larger left-leaning publishers (the ones one might expect to be Central's natural customers) to move to Central; they wanted to keep their radical politics, but combine this with secure, capitalist distribution; of course they had a point – the larger distributors might appear to give them an advantage in the market place, and Central was comparatively small and not without financial problems at the time. However, some of the larger distributors were to fail as several of these left-wing publishers found to their cost. Over the years, a number of large and well established distributors have gone under, not just the smaller, radical companies like PDC and Third World Distribution.

It has been helpful for Central to have a distinct identity, and not just be a general distributor, but adaptability and flexibility were essential. Central took on Semiotext, the interesting American post-modern political publishers in late 1985; this was an early sign of branching out. It was in the late 1980s that there was an expansion in the number and size of publishers that Central took on: Merlin Press, Monthly Review, Redstone Press, Child Poverty Action Group, Age Concern among others. It had taken Bill four years to find his feet and start signing up the new publishers that would ensure the transformation and survival of the company.

Some aspects of life continued as before, others were to change dramatically. Apart from the new publishers, other significant developments were in staff relations. Disputes did not disappear – they probably never will. There were occasionally serious arguments over whether some item should be distributed. In the days of apartheid in South Africa, arguments occurred over whether the boycott should be strictly adhered to, or Central should try to send political material both legally and illegally. The ANC were always consulted before any decision was taken. In 1988, staff voted to cease distribution of a journal called *The Fred* – probably over an explicit sexist cartoon, but memories are already hazy on that one. Other books were looked at from the same point of view, and it was decided to cease distributing one publisher entirely, mainly because of one book, that again had what most staff viewed as dubious visual material (this publisher moved to Turnaround, who had no such qualms). There was another serious dispute, this time over an order for half a dozen copies from the Kuwait Embassy for a book that was perceived as denying the holocaust.

There have always been differences between the cultures of office life and warehouse life – an upstairs/downstairs scenario, if you like. Originally, the warehouse staff would have been more working class; later there was a mix of students and part-time workers, then a bohemian element, and from the mid 1980s there has been a tendency for warehouse staff to be unusually well educated, even over-qualified, many having degrees. This is not a typical warehouse; there has been for some years now an amazingly high number of artists, critics, poets and musicians who have worked there.

It has often been the most overtly 'political' part of the company – in the 1970s/1980s there were always contingents from the warehouse on demonstrations, and political discussions raged most strongly in the warehouse, though this was always easier because of the way people worked in close proximity to each other. It is probably true to say that warehouse staff are better paid in relation to office staff than in other companies. Recent managers of the Despatch Department (David 'Harry' Crystal, and now Dave Williams) have made strong arguments for a starting wage that is the same in warehouse and office.

There were attempts to find new ways of involving staff in decision making – some were tentative, some did not really work (including, surprisingly, regular meetings for all members of staff; what happened was that discussions tended to be dominated by a small number of people).

In January 1986, the Directors rejected a proposal from the workforce for representation on the Board: the reply was 'the staff have always had the facility to put their requests to the Board'. What was suggested instead was a bi-monthly meeting between staff reps and two or three, members of the Board/management. But in December, after further discussion, a resolution was passed to have one worker rep on the Board. Some reps have been more confident than others in participating in discussion on the Board, but the experiment is positive. One interesting entry in the minutes, in November 1990, reads: 'The worker rep asked whether the Board could guarantee that no Poll Tax payments would be deducted from wages. Board members had different opinions on how far the company could go before being obliged to deduct from wages, but the consensus was that we should go as far as possible in delaying any such deductions but if the financial future of the company was threatened we would have to do it.'

In 1996, on the question of staff, there was, after much discussion, a significant restructuring of wages, which involved reducing the existing increments for length of service, and introducing new increments for responsibility. Prior to this, wage differentials in the company were extremely low, as already noted, and even now are not high.

One of the worker reps remarked at one Board meeting

that the company was becoming too management orientated; some decisions could be interpreted in this light: the introduction of clocking-in cards for all members of staff; the setting up of a Management Team to meet weekly in 1992; the creation of a Deputy Manager in the Despatch Department etc. But these decisions only indicated the slowness of management to introduce some necessary changes.

A major structural change in the company occurred when Democratic Left decided to divest itself of the companies that its predecessor, the Communist Party, had established many years earlier. It was certainly true that Farleigh Press (the CP printers), L&W and Central Books were no longer a source of income – if they ever had been. Democratic Left did not see itself as a political party, nor even as an organisation that wanted the responsibility of looking after these old fashioned companies. L&W and Central were asked to put forward plans for a transfer of ownership. L&W actually kept more formal links with DL, which remained a shareholder as did Central, and the Wishart family kept their traditional 20%. Central's proposal, which was accepted, involved the transfer of the shares to the current workforce, with all members of staff, who had worked there for four years or more, receiving some shares; the bulk went to members of the current management, on the basis of responsibility and length of service. DL was concerned that the company carried on in the same tradition and perspective, and it had confidence that the management would do that, but it also wanted to ensure that it would be difficult for any one individual or group to change the orientation of the company.

In the 1990s, a lot of time and effort went into the setting up of an Employees' Trust, which would divide the first £10,000 of any dividends equally between all members of staff, regardless of position, as long as they had worked for two years (part-timers would be paid pro-rata). It was finalised in September 1994. There had never been any dividends before, but the financial position was looking positive and, in 1996, a dividend was declared. There has been a dividend each year since, so everybody has benefited from an old capitalist practice, share dividends, though it can hardly be called 'unearned income'! Two members of the Trust are elected annually to the Board, replacing the former workers' rep.

Have these measures worked? Does everybody feel more involved in the company, or is it only the extra cash that matters? The answer is still open, but the effort is probably worthwhile.

Sales were increasing, but the period of crises was by no means over. Rents at the Leathermarket, as all over London at the time, were rising rapidly. In March of 1989, the landlords proposed a rent increase to £48,000; the company was offered £100,000 to sell the lease back, as this was the period of ridiculous property prices, and they had spectacular plans for redeveloping the site. The Board stuck out for more, and later in the year the offer went up to £250,000 ; this was an offer that couldn't be refused – in fact it was taken up just in time because, a few months later, the property market collapsed and the landlords went bankrupt. With the money (plus a mortgage) premises were bought at 99 Wallis Road in Hackney Wick, after Bill had scoured the East End for somewhere suitable. Single storey warehouses on the outskirts of London were considered, but with no enthusiasm. So was the Farleigh Press site in Watford – but this was 'impractical because of problems of staff travelling out so far'. Contracts were exchanged in June 1990; the building was in a poor state of repair and needed a lot of work done on it; the lowest bid (£80,000) was accepted, and the move took place in September 1990. Several largish publishers were considering Central for distribution at this time, but were worried about problems that might come with a change of premises.

Wallis Road is in a slightly run down industrial backwater of Hackney Wick – local facilities are non-existent, and certainly not as interesting as the London Bridge area where the Leathermarket was. However, access to the building was much better – an exterior hoist and then an inside lift were installed; the position meant Central could live up to its name. This proximity to central London was extremely useful in servicing an important number of customers, and over half of the staff lived in Hackney so they were happy.

The move cost £50,000 more than estimated, and cash-flow problems were developing. The CP had hiked the rent for Grays Inn Road up from the artificially low £3,500 to the more realistic, but impossible, £15,000. In 1991, Central got a loan of £50,000 from Democratic Left (ironically cash rich for such a small, radical organisation) with interest and a charge on the building; this loan stabilised the company. A condition attached to the loan was that the shop be given a month to produce plans to show it could break even. The losses at the shop had been causing concern for a while, and the fear was that it could bring the whole company down. Still, the vote to close the shop was only three to two in favour (with two new directors at their first meeting abstaining). It was a very sad decision to have to take – it ended a period of 70 years during which the CP had had a public face in the form of a retail shop. It closed in March 1992, and got a small obituary in The Independent. Grays Inn Road was not a brilliant site for a bookshop: although public transport was good, parking was bad (this would be more of a problem from the 1970s onwards). The area may have had an interesting radical pedigree, but not many people lived locally, passing trade was limited, and the bookshop never catered to the local community of lawyers. The proximity of The Times and Sunday Times in Grays Inn Road brought some business (striking staff there were given free use of a room in the 1970s), but then high hopes of the new ITN building in the 1980s were to be disappointed in terms of extra trade.

The shop was very small initially, as the back of the ground floor was used as a picking area for the distribution of books and magazines (this was later to be filled with second hand books). When the warehouse moved to the

top **Office at the Leathermarket –
Mark Chilver, Peter Kelly and
Bill Norris 1990**
above **A few days later, Bill takes
last orders at the Leathermarket**

Leathermarket in 1978, the shop expanded right back, and the office was in the charming extension with a glass roof that will be remembered with affection by all who worked there, and by reps who came – though it's true that it could be extremely hot in summer and leaks in wet weather were not unknown (the CP's handyman, Reg, was often employed on the roof there). Given the curious layout of the shop with its nooks and crannies and unoccupied rooms, security was a problem: books, and on rarer occasions, money disappeared with depressing regularity.

However, the shop became very well known – even abroad – and had many devoted customers; in its own way, it had become a minor institution and was genuinely mourned. Some real characters were to be found working in the shop – Bill Allen and Jack Berlin spring to mind. Bill, who appeared earlier in the narrative worried about his age, was a former preacher ('defrocked for honourable political reasons', says Arthur Mendelsohn); Jack was notorious for his rudeness to customers and colleagues but was at the same time a much loved man. The retail side of the business was always better known than the distribution side – it was the more public face of the company. Even today many people do not realise that Central Books still exists – they think it went with the shop. There was some continuity from Grays Inn Road, with the mail order side of the business being transferred to Wallis Road, with Peter Logan, and this has been expanded in recent years; the second-hand stock from the shop was taken on by 'Left on the Shelf', so there is some continuation of the retail business there too.

In 1993 there was an injunction from the publisher John Calder relating to one of Central's publishers who shouldn't have published a Samuel Beckett novel, as there was a dispute over the rights – this was the second tussle with the man, the first being in 1959.

Wage increases were very low at this time, but there were built in guaranteed increments for length of service, so it wasn't too bad for staff. There is an interesting analysis to be done of wage levels in radical bookshops: a lot only survived because of the deep level of voluntary self-exploitation by the people running them; wages and conditions were accepted that were denounced in books and pamphlets sold by these shops. 'All for the cause' was the reply and it is true – it was dedication, not financial reward, that kept them going. This is partly true of Central as well, though it was easier in London than in other cities and towns, and the backing of a political party was helpful overall (although non-aligned bookshops could appeal more easily for grants, donations and assistance).

A major feature of Central's business has been the distribution of magazines. Some of the small left-wing journals, like those originally carried, are still there (*Labour Research* was on the list in 1939 and is still there), but this has broadened out in a similar way to the book publishers. Central supply the book trade (as well as galleries for art magazines like *Modern Painters*, *Art Review*, *Art Monthly* etc, wholefood shops and other outlets for green and alternative mags – *Food Magazine*, *Resurgence* etc), but not the news trade, which is another type of business altogether. Bookshops have not traditionally given much attention to magazines – they take up valuable space, there's not much profit in them as they are so cheap, they can be time-consuming to return etc.) – and many shops do not bother at all. But those that do, find magazines can bring in regular customers, and some of the new superstores are installing huge magazine and journal sections. Its tradition of selling small quantities of mags to lots of different outlets was the basis for Central to develop this side of the business, and now it is known as the largest, and most effective, distributor of magazines to bookshops. They range from literary titles, like the *London Review of Books*, *Literary Review* and the *T.L.S.* that fit easily into bookshops, to academic journals. Subject matter includes: film, music, cultural studies, philosophy, design, feminist, gay, third world, history, etc. The magazines come from all over the world, they are not limited to the UK. Even with the recent expansion, the magazine trade has kept up: it has been about 25% of the business for two decades now.

The political profile of the company changed somewhat, but did not disappear. CB did turn away publishers who would not fit in; a largish vanity publisher comes to mind, but there are others which would not be accepted for producing fascist, racist, sexist or homophobic literature. In the shop, there was a big political debate about whether to stock an Irish Republican paper – in the end it was taken. However, there was one notorious internal factional paper published secretly by unnamed CP members, *The Leninist*, that Central refused to stock, but it was unreadable anyway. Despite this, there is no doubt that Central's recent history is one of welcoming political pluralism. The shop stocked all the Trotskyist and other far left papers, though occasionally an obscure one published by Peruvian Maoists, or a small group nobody had heard of working from a PO Box number in Merioneth, would denounce us for not stocking their four page duplicated sheet that came out every four and half months. On these occasions the shop would ring to shrill accusations of Stalinism, and ordinary customers would cower in the second hand department – or join in!

The perception of Central Books in some eyes had not changed for decades: as far as the extreme right was concerned it was a legitimate target. The shop, like many left bookshops, had been attacked by fascists in the early 1980s (windows broken, an arson attempt in March 1982), at the time of a resurgence in their activity throughout the country; in 1993 a fascist leaflet threatened Board members, and the company's premises, though a crude map, intended to show its position, pinpointed the local greasy spoon café. The police did take these threats seriously and were very helpful with security advice.

Communist literature was not selling: in 1986 the minutes note 'General downturn in sales to Party outlets are a

Publicity material was more professional in the 1980s

worrying problem'. The number of CP shops at this time was probably half a dozen. The Communist Party ceased to exist after its 43rd Congress in November 1991 – the majority of what remained of the membership forming Democratic Left; and, if it is of any academic historical interest, the two remaining members of the CP at Central – the MD and company secretary – joined DL.

The company certainly became much more business-like in the late 1980s/1990s. The work of Mark Chilver as Sales Manager and Director, from March 1993, was crucial in helping turn the company round (he was also to become the key IT person). Contracts with publishers were improved. A proper Management Team was set up. Central started attending the Frankfurt and London Bookfairs – this was much appreciated by the smaller publishers, who did not have the resources to go themselves (especially to the London one which is much more expensive than Frankfurt). Publicity material became much more professional (Kirstie Kemp did a lot in this area), and the quality of reports to publishers increased significantly. The Board was extended to include people with a wide range of experience in the book trade – previously the only director who did not work at the company was Sally Davison. It was a significant advance when the manager of the Despatch Department was automatically made a Board member.

A part-time magazine rep was appointed, initially with the help of a grant from the Arts Council, which was searching for ways to help small literary and art magazines to extend their circulation, and to become more self-sufficient. Distribution has always been a major problem for small publishers; the company was pleased to be involved in discussions with the Arts Council, as it was a recognition of its achievements, and a lot of time and effort was put into this.

In 1988, it was decided to use Troika for book representation. Central had changed its position on repping many times over the years; there had been one rep in 1946 (Max Goldberg) though later that year there was a part time rep for Cobbett Press (a short-lived CP publishing enterprise) in London, and it had remained a subject for continual discussion. From the mid 1990s, there was an increase in the number of different repping companies used (though this was ultimately the publishers' decision); some of these companies brought new publishers (as Troika had) – this did, however, work in reverse: when a publisher changed reps they sometimes changed distributor.

Staff training was seriously looked at. In another step which reflected the greatly improved financial position, it was felt more that than lip service could be paid to the belief that the staff that was the company's main asset: a Group Pension Scheme was started. An attempt was made to give some financial recognition to the responsibilities that people had taken on, to the flexibility that they had shown, acknowledging that, in a company as small as Central, there is always going to be limited room for promotion. The length of service of some members of staff has already been mentioned; as well as these, in 1999, Peter Logan has been here 15 years, and the head of the accounts department, Hamid Moheebob, usually known as Bob, 20 years. Management tried to be flexible on working hours and accommodate requests by members of staff to change their working week, or change to working part-time, e.g. on becoming parents, on taking up further education, on taking up voluntary work etc.

Reflecting on this recent period, which I can write about from personal experience as well as from the recollections of others, and the often minimal minutes (I joined the Board at the end of 1984, started work in Grays Inn Road in 1987, and became company secretary in 1988), the most obvious change is the turnover. Sales in 1984,85 and 86 were static at £650,000 but then rose by an average of roughly £150,000 a year, to reach over £3,000,000 last year (in this period turnover declined in only one year). As a distributor, there is a limit to what one can do to increase turnover: it largely depends on what the publishers produce for sale, plus their marketing, the repping and the state of the retail trade. Here the development of the retail chains really helped, though, ironically, this contributed to the decline of what had once been the core customer base – the radical bookshops (today there are less than ten, three of which are in London). There has been no growth of any other sort of 'alternative' bookshop: black bookshops rose and declined at the same time as the left-wing ones; purely women's bookshops could only ever survive in London, and even then with difficulty. There is no group of anarchist or green bookshops, but green books and magazines are sold in a range of health food shops. The days are well gone when a city like Liverpool could support, in the mid/late 1970s, a Communist, two Trotskyist, a Maoist and a very good general radical bookshop (with an anarchist/feminist orientation). In fact, one of the current trends in the book trade is the demise of the independent general bookshop; this kind of shop, however much loved and rooted in the community, just does not have the resources and clout to compete with the chains.

The Soviet connection declined rapidly in this period; in 1990 the consignment arrangement with MK ended - all purchases would be firm sale – but it was too late for them to act like a normal business. It was in March 1992, after the collapse of the Soviet Union, that the Board 'recognised that the MK link is over'.

Of course, if the publisher base had not been broadened, Central would not have survived to celebrate this anniversary. Incidentally, a similar transformation occurred at L&W, which moved from being largely a publisher of traditional Marxist material, labour movement history and some radical fiction, to include a wider range of political books and journals, notably in the field of cultural politics. The smaller radical publishers, who came to Central with the demise of PDC, could not have provided enough turnover. Central Books had the skills and knowledge, as well as the practical necessities in terms of computers and warehouse space, to take on a new range of publishers. The majority of new publishers came on board because of Central's reputation and flexibility. Publishers change distributors warily, which is quite understandable given the risk for a publisher if they make a bad decision, or if the distributor has problems. A good distributor is essential to the health of the publisher. Some of the publishers who came in the 1980s have moved on – some for good reasons (or understandable ones!), and others possibly made a mistake in leaving.

Reputation is crucial – despite the increasing concentration in publishing, as well as retailing, it remains an industry where individuals are very important: many of our publishers are owned or run by one person. For us, at Central, it is Bill who has done the lion's share of negotiating and building up relations with publishers, and his achievements here have been fundamental to the success of the company over this period. His accessibility, and the time he has spent talking to publishers, advising and helping them, is readily recognised and appreciated – perhaps in a larger company this is just not possible.

Some publishers left, but a lot more have stayed, and hopefully have benefited from the company's consolidation and expansion. The profile of the publishers handled has obviously varied over the years. Lawrence and Wishart has been distributed continuously for the 60 years; today there are other political publishers such as Merlin, Monthly Review, and newer ones like Porcupine, who see Central as a natural home in a historical sense – it has not given up trying to help publishers of Marxist works, though the market has shrunk. There are the campaigning charitable publishers like the Child Poverty Action Group, Amnesty International, the Commission for Racial Equality, Minority Rights Group, Charities Aid Foundation, Disability Alliance. There are several green publishers, like Jon Carpenter Publishing, there is a more recent group of think tanks (IPPR, Demos, Centre for Policy on Ageing, SMF) – CB is close to having a monopoly. There are several interesting literary publishers – Dedalus, Oberon, Totterdown, Pulp Faction; there are half a dozen Irish publishers (and one Welsh one – Seren); there are quite a number of smaller academic publishers – including University Presses such as Hertfordshire, Middlesex, Birmingham, LSE. There are some foreign university presses, among a batch of significant third world publishers, some imported by the Africa Book Centre, others home-grown, like New Internationalist. There are feminist publishers, and there is a strong gay presence with GMP and Prowler Press. There are some classy cookery publishers (Prospect, Absolute), several art and film publishers (Redstone, Hyphen, 21) and, of course, some general publishers (Broadcast, Serif, Westworld International, Politico's among others). What may appear a rather curious area of specialisation, was the taking on of several interesting Islamic publishers, on the liberal, or Sufi side, it must be said. It's unlikely any of the more fundamentalist ones would have tolerated CB distributing Salman Rushdie's *Satanic Verses* when, in 1994, the consortium of publishers who printed the paperback edition approached the company, at the time of the threats against publishers and retailers of the book. This was such an important issue that there was a full staff meeting to discuss the matter, and everyone wanted to distribute it.

The aim here is not just to give a plug to a small selection of the 350 publishers of books and magazines that Central distributes – though I am happy to do this, and I'm sorry I can't mention more – but it is to indicate the continuity and change in the portfolio of publishers handled. CB has gone out of its way to provide a service to smaller, independent publishers especially those who do represent an alternative, or ethical, approach to the problems the world faces. In some ways, that misused, or misunderstood, word 'stakeholder' is relevant, though the company has veered away from the 'mission statement' syndrome. Central Books is clear it has a stake in the well-being of Hackney and would like, at least in some small way, to put something back into the local community – the company is represented on the Wick Regeneration Board. I hope this brief account shows the importance of ensuring that both the staff and the publishers have a stake in the company, and one of the purposes of this history is to ensure that those who built up the company over the past 60 years - the historical stakeholders – are remembered. There is no problem attempting to marry good business practice with this ethical approach, and hopefully this can continue into the new millennium. Roll on the next 60 years!